SURVIVING A UNIVERSITY DEPARTMENT FROM HELL

An Exposé of the University of Cape Town (UCT)

By
NDANGWA NOYOO

Surviving a University Department from Hell:
An Exposé of the University of Cape Town (UCT)

Published by Southern African Policy and
Development Nexus (SAPDN)

Cape Town, South Africa

info@sapdnafrica.co.za

ISBN 979-8-22313924-9

2 4 6 8 10 9 7 5 3 1

Layout and cover design by Boutique Books

Printed in South Africa by Bidvest Data

DEDICATION

I dedicate this book to my beautiful and wonderful children. I also dedicate this work to all black African academics who continue to be made invisible as well as denigrated by some racist universities in South Africa.

CONTENTS

A book of this nature usually generates different and strong views, emotions and stances. Some may easily dismiss it as "sour grapes" or even a "rant", while others may effortlessly resonate with it because it may speak to their experiences, daily lived realities, lamentations or even horrors in the different academic spaces across South Africa where they ply their trade. Even at a personal level, it can open spaces for random individuals to offer their unsolicited, "I know him," comments, to anyone, based on a fleeting interaction they may have had with you some thirty-plus years ago.

Writing this book was not something I even contemplated during my five and a half years of torment at the University of Cape Town (UCT). I had subjected myself to various kangaroo courts, which were convened by different senior managers in a certain faculty, which were meant to either terminate my employment or squeeze me out of UCT. In fact, the prime motive for such arbitrary and Gestapo-inspired processes was the need to protect six under performing academics in the department I was working in.

I responded to these sham and biased processes with the attitude of "being the bigger person" and firmly believed that due process had to unfold so that justice could be served. Such thinking was tempered by my firm belief that I was following university policies and procedures, and was adhering to my key performance areas (KPAs) and that it would be easy for all to see that I was doing my job. However, the more I was subjected to these sham processes, the more I lost confidence in them. Shockingly, I would deduce that they were used by some people at UCT to punish those who refused to be their cronies or lackeys and who just wanted to get on with the task of focussing on the academic project.

The "light bulb" moment to write this book was triggered after I had received an extremely vexing and bizarre email from UCT management, which was meant to coerce me into attending an unjust disciplinary process, and on my birthday for that matter. I refused. This was the last straw, and I was not going to be cowed, harassed or intimidated anymore by a racist and callous system. Enough was enough, I said to myself. Thus, I drew the proverbial line in the sand. Let them come, I thought. They can fire me. I am fed up! After receiving this highly questionable communication from management and the Human Resources (HR) department of UCT, I said to myself, no man, this is not right! I cannot continue to be treated like a dog after all I have done for this university! Even a dog deserves dignity and to be treated well. Really? I then made the resolute decision to expose the rot at UCT, the consequences be damned!

Why and how did I arrive at this militant decision? What drove me to this position where I was compelled to expose a university I was associated with for six and a half years? After five and half years of being hounded by so-called workmates, who were heavily and overtly backed by senior managers at faculty level and HR officials, I felt like a wounded buffalo and knew I had nothing to lose. Also, I was painfully aware that their campaign against me was fuelled by hatred, petty jealousy and other sinister motives I will not dwell on here. Crucially, it was based on lies, conjecture and hearsay. That is why they could not remove me from UCT, despite trying for a whole period of five and a half years.

     Surviving a University Department from Hell

I, on the other hand, had overwhelming evidence against them and had marshalled the former and brought it to every kangaroo court UCT convened against me. After I had provided such evidence, I had left the conveners of such processes smarting and angry. In normal circumstances, they would have acted on what I had brought them and disciplined these rogue academics. However, this was not the case and would not be. Also, in normal circumstances, they would have stopped this vicious and evil campaign against me. But this was anything but normal. They kept on coming after me like a pack of wild dogs.

It was wave after wave of attack, for a whole, solid five and a half years! The last harassment from the university management and HR was informed by their desire to force me to recognise and defer to one of the individuals in a group of six individuals, who had hounded me in the said period, and who was also their leader. This individual, even though he was involved in an incident of burning an office and also used intoxicating substances at the workplace, had never faced any disciplinary action from the university management.

While I was the Head of Department (HoD), I caught him red-handed in the morning, intoxicated on substances. I was not the only one who found him "high as a kite" early in the morning. There were four other UCT officials with me, namely a health and safety officer, the said department's senior administrator and two campus protection services (CPS) officers. This was exactly one week after he had burnt an office due to his smoking of drugs at the workplace. Previously, another staff member had complained to me about his smoking of drugs in his office. Moreover, it was an open secret in both the department and university that this man smoked drugs at the workplace. But all the wrong things that this individual had done did not matter because they promoted him to the position of HoD. In fact, they rewarded his criminal behaviour while I was squeezed out of the headship.

When this individual burnt an office, he was supposed to have been on sabbatical. However, he was always at UCT, mounting a vicious campaign against me, together with his five conspirators, trying to oust me from the position of HoD while smoking drugs in a small office downstairs, which was meant for student supervision. He did this because he felt that it was his God-given right to be an HoD. And after two and a half years of this diabolical and well-orchestrated scheme, he managed to drive me out of my position with the help of some senior managers. But this individual and his cohorts would not stop there, as they were baying for my blood and continued with this evil scheme, even when I stepped down as HoD. This would be for another three and a half years.

It is interesting to note that his burning of the office and the discovery of drug paraphernalia were ably captured by CPS in their arson report pertaining to the fire incident in the Robert Leslie Social Science (RLSS) building in October 2018, after an earlier investigation was concluded by CPS. To date, no one has been brought to book for this crime. Although the CPS had fingered the said individual as the most likely perpetrator of this crime, UCT management and HR went out of their way to protect him and continue to do so at all costs. Instead of instituting disciplinary action against the culprit or, better still, reporting this crime to the South African Police Service (SAPS), they came after me with all sorts of ill-conceived "disciplinary actions". This behaviour by UCT management and HR is not only shocking and shameful, but it is scandalous!

What did they actually do? Well, first, the university management and HR sought to dispel the arson – as if the fire had just started itself. Then they tried to bury it or cover it up. Before I left UCT, they were trying to delegitimise the arson report and exonerate the said individual (through a cover up type of "investigation") while instituting a "disciplinary action" against me for refusing to take an instruction from someone I believe is a drug addict and arsonist.

Under normal circumstances, this man should have been fired a long time ago. But here we were, five years later, and I was again facing trumped up charges because of trying to expose this type of criminal behaviour; for basically doing my job. If it had been a white HoD who had reported an errant black African academic, I am pretty sure that first, management and HR would have supported him or her and pulled out all the stops, and second, the black African man or woman would have been fired with immediate effect! That is why I was not prepared to go through another useless and sinister so-called disciplinary process which was solely aimed at squeezing me out of UCT. I thus decided to leave UCT.

I would like the reader to indulge me here, for just a minute. Try to put yourself in my shoes. What would you have done when your co-worker, whom you'd found intoxicated on drugs or whatever, and whom you'd reported to management, was made your HoD? This man was forced on the few of us who did not subscribe to the corrupt agenda of UCT's management and HR.

This time, I was ready to leave the highly toxic and vile environment of UCT. Truthfully, I have never worked at such a venomous, evil and toxic place in my whole working life! Never! When I left the University of Johannesburg (UJ) in 2017, I thought I was going to the "Number One" university in Africa. All I found at UCT was mediocrity, disrespect and corruption. This is how I experienced UCT. Do not get me wrong: there are other areas of UCT where there is cutting-edge research and where academic excellence abounds. Probably, these are the sections of the university that are contributing to UCT's "Number One" status. However, in my case, my six and a half years at UCT were nothing but a nightmare, exemplified by corruption, mediocrity, thuggish behaviour and so forth.

Some of the issues I raise, report on, or discuss in this book may seem like pure fiction to serious-minded people. In fact, even as I was writing this book, I was shocked all over again at the things that were happening in an institution of higher learning, almost thirty years into democracy. I will highlight and tabulate more of these highly questionable activities, peddled by mainly six academics who made torturing me their favourite game. By the time I have finished unpacking some of the things I encountered or had to deal with, the reader may think that I am exaggerating (if you are a die-hard fan of UCT) or infuriated (if you are not the former).

I do not think that there can be a middle ground for the things that I raise in this exposé. Why have I chosen the route of an exposé and not just resigning and quietly leaving UCT? This is usually what happens when black African academics, who have had a run-in with UCT, leave this institution. It seems UCT has become adept at treating those who have crossed paths with its functionaries shabbily and cruelly. Some who left the university sought "to put the nightmare behind them". I almost did this. However, after I saw how management and HR had fast-tracked the so-called disciplinary action against me, brought by someone I firmly believe is an arsonist and drug addict, as well as an illegitimate HoD, I was not only infuriated, but I was instantly taken back to my radical and militant student days where, in radical parlance, we would say, "Hell, let us burn down this unjust system!"

And that is what I am doing in this book. I am burning down the pernicious and corrosive UCT system! However, my main intention is not only to expose the rot and oppressive system at UCT. I am writing this book for my children so that they know that their father stood firm against a corrupt and oppressive university and for black African academics and students who continue to be made "invisible" by an uncaring academic system that is underpinned by patriarchy, white privilege, white hegemony and an arrogant sense of white entitlement.

Earlier this year (2023), one of my vocal third year students asked me whether education was a right or privilege. I was surprised by his question, but I answered him that it was a right. He noted that this was something that had been debated in a forum he had participated in. This is the thinking or attitude I find being extended to black African academics at UCT. "They must be grateful to find themselves in such a place" goes the colonial and apartheid paradigm, which is still entrenched at UCT. If you dare question some malpractices happening at this university, then you will feel the wrath of UCT.

I will return to these issues and substantively flesh them out in Chapters One and Two.

I am writing this book on the back of unceremonious departures of the immediate past Vice Chancellor (VC) and the Head of the Council of the university. Both are black African women with impeccable academic credentials, but they were hastily and shabbily ejected from UCT, for reasons best known to the university. At the centre of the saga that led to the departure of these black African women is a white deputy vice chancellor (DVC), whose word seemed to have been taken as gospel truth by a predominantly white Senate and other UCT structures. I had previously crossed paths with this DVC because of the six belligerent lecturers and a dean of a certain faculty. In my dealings with her, she had shown clear partiality and sided with the foregoing individuals. I had reported to her the arson incident and singled out the individual at the centre of the fire in RLSS, as well as other unsavoury actions by the said individual and his cohorts, towards me. She merely scoffed at me. However, when she had snuck her "grievance" through the back door of Senate, she was painted as a saint by the retrogressive sections of UCT and biased white media.

On the other hand, the former VC was easily considered a *bête noire* in this tussle. I will return to these issues in the next section. What I want to point out here is that not only did the former DVC support the man I consider a drug addict and arsonist, by not taking any disciplinary action against him, but she and the dean promoted him and made him an HoD. Curiously, the individual I consider a drug addict and arsonist formed part of a group of academics who had raised "serious concerns" related to governance matters under the leadership of the former VC in one Senate session. Talk about the kettle calling the pot black! I doubt if the evidence against the VC is like what I have seen: an arson report based on a thorough investigation by CPS, with close circuit television (CCTV) footage and several eyewitness accounts.

In my experience at UCT, I think that allegations can be treated as true accounts, depending on who was making them

   Surviving a University Department from Hell

and who was being accused. I later discovered when I became an HoD that anyone could stand up and declare that he or she had been "bullied", and the onus would be on the accused to prove otherwise. In effect, one would be deemed guilty and had to prove one's innocence and not the other way round. Hence, the onus was on me to prove that I did not "bully" anyone. Nevertheless, it is important to note that the violent removal from office of these two eminent black African women and their public humiliation sends a powerful message to young black African women of South Africa. Whether they were culpable or not the question is, what does this say for female black African leadership in higher education?

From my childhood and over the years, I was told that hard work pays, and the merit system is the gold standard in life. Not at UCT! At least, not from my experience. What I saw was that mediocrity and cronyism were handsomely rewarded. No matter how hard I worked for UCT, all I got in return was disdain, insults and shabby treatment. I had never experienced anything of this nature in all my working life.

Personally, I have benefited a lot from the merit system. For example, I won a prestigious scholarship in 1994 to go and study at the University of Cambridge. I did not just wake up one day and decided to go and study at Cambridge, where I obtained a master's degree in 1995, but earned that opportunity. Where would I have conjured up such a dream? Equally, where would I (and students from several Commonwealth countries) have had the rare opportunity of meeting and mingling with then Prince Charles?

At the time, being young and quite impetuous, a fellow student from Africa and I had prepped ourselves beforehand to give Prince Charles an icy response when and if he greeted us. I must say, after seeing how he mingled with us young students and, to my disbelief, how unpretentious he seemed, I was quite disarmed. Now he is the king of England. I asked myself this question when he became the king of England: Where would have I met this man if it had not been for education and the scholarship that facilitated my move to the United Kingdom and the University of Cambridge? Prince Charles was the patron of the Cambridge Commonwealth Trust Fund.

Apart from being guided by the merit system, I have always loved scholarly work since I was at nursery school. Even as a child, I knew what I wanted when it came to education. I loved school and always wanted to pursue scholarly activities from my formative years. I was very clear on this. I could not wait to start school, especially when I watched my elder siblings go to school every morning in their neat and well pressed uniforms! Thus, I worked hard to get where I am today, believing that there are no short-cuts in academia or even in life, for that matter.

As a young person, I was inspired by Africa's deep thinkers, as well as those from other parts of the world. Hence, I did not just stumble into academia or want to be an academic for any other reason than for the pursuit of knowledge and disseminating it in a less esoteric way. This is the first time in my life that I do not have any appetite for academic engagements – all thanks to UCT. I need to pause and begin my healing process.

This is not the first time that UCT is being exposed by an academic. Others and more eminent than me, such as the renowned professor Jonathan Jensen from the University of

     Surviving a University Department from Hell

Stellenbosch, have done so with dexterity. However, this is the first time, I think, it is being done by someone who was heading a department and wanted to effect change and transform it from a lackadaisical department into a premier academic entity. Also, this is not the first time that UCT has ill-treated a black African scholar like me. Others with more pedigree have suffered similar fates.

The esteemed and highly acclaimed black scholar Mahmood Mamdani suffered shabby treatment at the hands of UCT. In September 1996, he was appointed to the Archibald Campbell (AC) Jordan Chair in African studies at UCT and became director of the Centre for African Studies in early 1997. In October that year, he submitted the outline of the core course for the foundation semester for first-year social science and humanities students. However, the curriculum planning committee could not reach consensus over the proposed curriculum and pedagogy, and he was suspended from the committee. The faculty rejected the course.

What the university now calls a "heated falling-out" became known as the "Mamdani affair". It prompted the scholar to ask, in a 1998 paper: "Is African studies to be turned into a new home for Bantu education at UCT?"[1] Mamdani would return to UCT to deliver a lecture on Decolonising the Post-colonial University, twenty years after he left because of the clash with the curriculum committee over his proposed core course on Africa. Mamdani revealed, when somebody asked him why he'd

---

1   Smit, S. (2018). *20 years after the 'Mamdani affair', the old adversary rejoins UCT*. Retrieved from https://mg.co.za/article/2018-06-05-20-years-after-the-mamdani-affair-the-old-adversary-rejoins-uct/

decided to come back after staying away from UCT for so long, "because 'Rhodes fell'."[2]

I want to slightly disagree with Professor Mamdani here. The statue of Cecil John Rhodes may have been removed from the UCT grounds, but what it symbolised – patriarchy, white privilege and white hegemony – are firmly rooted at UCT and embedded in all facets of its operations. "Transformation" and "decolonisation" remain hollow slogans at UCT. Furthermore, it is important to note that corruption is also thriving at UCT. That is why I find Professor Jansen's book on corruption at universities instructive. It alerts us to corruption and skulduggery at universities, where deep thinking and knowledge production are being sidelined while the academic project is becoming bleary and not easily discernible with each passing year.[3]

In my book, I foreground my experiences as a way of allowing the reader to see how things are so wrong at a university that has been touted as the "Number One" university in Africa. This book is for the silent majority of black Africans at institutions such as UCT in South Africa, where different rules apply to white and black African academics.

I think that I am fairly accomplished as an academic. If I can be treated with such indignity and disdain by UCT management and HR, just to protect some non-performing lecturers and an individual guilty of criminal behaviour, what might they do to

---

2 Omoyele, I. (2017). *Post-colonial universities are trapped by their past.* Retrieved from https://mg.co.za/article/2017-08-31-00-post-colonial-universities-are-trapped-by-their-past/
3 See Jansen, J. D. (2023). *Corrupted: A study of chronic dysfunction in South African universities.* Wits University Press.

   Surviving a University Department from Hell

someone who is young and still learning the ropes of academia and with whom they do not resonate? That is why I thought that it was important to write a book of this nature and expose the rot at UCT. I neither signed any non-disclosure agreement (NDA) nor received a "golden handshake" to muzzle me. Thus, it felt imperative to write a personal account of how I had experienced the various underhand machinations at UCT, in the form of an exposé and deal with whatever comes after this action.

Crucially, despite all my detractors not having any shred of evidence that I had sought to "bully" or "intimidate" them, they were pampered and listened to by senior managers at faculty level. "Lack of collegiality" was taken as a "serious allegation", which warranted my dismissal for five and half years. Not the burning of an office or smoking drugs at the workplace – this was not even considered a "serious allegation" – nor delving into the most intimate thoughts of young and unsuspecting students, in the guise of "counselling" them and then using that information to leverage them.

"Collegiality" was only defined from the position of one group of lecturers. It did not matter if these individuals insulted me, were nasty to me or constantly provoked me. I must add that there was another group of lecturers and colleagues with whom I worked well and who helped me to navigate the department in very turbulent and rough times. We did such great work together.

I want categorically to make it clear that all I have reported in this book is true and the contents can be corroborated with the evidence I have, as well as by eyewitnesses and from personal accounts of people who were associated with the department in question. It is my fervent hope that students and lecturers who have been ill-treated, abused and demonised by certain individuals from this department will also come forward and provide their own versions of the maleficence that was spearheaded by this department for many years.

This book is discussed in five chapters. The first chapter locates my discussions in the broader context of higher education in South Africa in the post-apartheid era. In this section, I argue that universities are the last bastion of patriarchy, white privilege and white hegemony. Therefore, the intense contestation that we are witnessing across South Africa is symptomatic of a vested section of society fighting tooth and nail not to lose its dominance in this sector, by any means at its disposal. As the adage goes, knowledge is power. White academics have seen patriarchy, white privilege and white hegemony whittled away across the country over almost three decades. This sector seems to be their last stand, and they will do anything to protect their dominant position in institutions of higher learning, especially universities.

Chapter Two is titled *Arrival and Initial Shock*. In this chapter I describe my arrival at UCT and my initial shock after discovering some malpractices in the department in which I was working, which seemed to be deemed as normal by the people I was working with.

Chapter Three casts light on my tenure as HoD until I was hounded from this position. I detail some of the shocking things that happened to me and that I was subjected to, with no consequences whatsoever for the perpetrators. In fact, they were supported by some senior managers at faculty level.

Chapter Four focusses on the elevation of the faction that ousted me into positions of influence by senior managers in

     Surviving a University Department from Hell

the faculty. This chapter details how the said individuals sought to break my spirit and totally humiliate me. The chapter also casts light on the shenanigans that led to my resolute decision to refuse to be demeaned and oppressed anymore by some individuals at UCT, as well as informed my decision to leave the university.

Chapter Five concludes the book.

Ndangwa Noyoo
Cape Town, South Africa
2023

ACADEMIA IN POST-APARTHEID SOUTH AFRICA: THE LAST BASTION OF PATRIARCHY, WHITE PRIVILEGE AND WHITE HEGEMONY

My first forays into academia in South Africa were at the University of the Witwatersrand (Wits) in Johannesburg in 1997. During this period, the ripples of what was known as the "Makgoba affair" were still being felt across this university and the country. Prega Govender reports in the Mail and Guardian that in 1996, after Malegapuru Makgoba, who later became the University of KwaZulu-Natal's vice-chancellor – known then as William Makgoba – was appointed deputy vice-chancellor of Wits, a magnificently bruising row broke out between him and thirteen academics. They alleged that Makgoba had essentially embellished his curriculum vitae (CV). In turn, he accessed their personal records and aired their dirty laundry in public, branding them racists. The affair eventually died down, with Makgoba leaving for the South African Medical Research Council, but the frailty of Wits seemed to linger, and it never quite recovered from the punch-up.[4]

I was recruited by a white South African HoD of British descent to drive his agenda of transforming a certain School at Wits. This was also during the period when this HoD was about to retire. In all my interactions with him, his motives pertaining to transformation seemed genuine. I still have a lot of respect for

---

4   Govender, P. (2013). *The healing of a divided Wits is Habib's mission.* Retrieved from https://www.timeslive.co.za/sunday-times/ lifestyle/2013-06-16-the-healing-of-a-divided-wits-is-habibs-mission/

this white academic, who passed away in 2016. This statement is made in the light of my views and perceptions regarding white people in this book and elsewhere. As I have mentioned previously and in other fora, some of the most wonderful people I've met in my life are white people. These people, including my nursery schoolteachers, who were missionaries of some sort, added value to my life and contributed to the sum of the person I am today. Therefore, I do not have any problem with white people *per se*. What I have a problem with is a vile, ignorant, arrogant and racist white person who thinks that I should not be part of humanity. That, I fundamentally have a problem with, and I do not care who such a person is. I will take him or her on if he or she comes after me. It is as simple as that.

Unfortunately, South Africa has not rid itself of its racist past, which keeps rearing its ugly head in all facets of its life. Academic life and academia in general are not immune to this scourge. If we look at the academic project in post-1994 South Africa, I would argue that it did not entirely take off after the fall of colonialism and apartheid. This is because there were a lot of carry-overs from the past order and thus efforts to transform the country and institutions of higher education by the new and first African government, which was led by the African National Congress (ANC), were not as radical and bold as in other African countries when they had attained independence. Arguably, the ANC's hands were tied behind its back because it had secured the country's freedom through a negotiated settlement, the hallmark of which was the *sunset clause*.[5]

---

5   South Africa's liberation was realised via a negotiated settlement and the sunset clause, which guaranteed certain rights and privileges to the former oppressors, was the pillar of such a settlement.

                                 Surviving a University Department from Hell

In short, black African scholars did not shape the national narrative in the way that African scholars, for instance, spearheaded the post-colonial African discourse, especially in the "Golden Era" of the 1960s and 1970s. In the said periods, African scholars were involved in academic pursuits that aimed at, among other issues, creating new post-colonial societies. Theory building, research or the teaching and learning environment were meant to foster new conditions of prosperity on the African continent, and these would result in the creation of a new African citizen, who had been unshackled from colonial servitude and was able to rise above everything and be counted as a human being who had a lot to contribute to world progress.

Part of this higher education in the "Golden Era" was meant to mentally liberate Africans and make them proud and confident in their own skins. This is the period when intellectual giants such as, *inter alia*, Walter Rodney, the author of the seminal book *How Europe Undeveloped Africa*, was teaching at the University of Dar es Salaam, Ali Mazrui at Makerere University, Wole Soyinka at the University of Ibadan, Samir Amin at the University of Dakar, Claude Ake at the Universities of Dar es Salaam, Nairobi and Port Harcourt, Cheikh Anta Diop at the University of Dakar, Dani Wadada Nabudere at the University of Dar es Salaam, and Paul Mwaipaya, Bernard Magubane and Ben Turok at the University of Zambia. Notwithstanding this gender bias, many African scholars were immersed in the task of creating a new post-colonial order and working tirelessly to develop and deepen African epistemologics.

In post-apartheid South Africa, scholarship was couched in the nebulous term of "transformation" and seemed to be driven mainly by white liberals who had their own views on what post-apartheid South Africa should look like. When the first democratically elected president Nelson Mandela vacated the political stage, it seemed quite curious at the time that some black African academics and intellectuals incessantly, and at times virulently, criticised his successor, former president Thabo Mbeki, without proffering any policy or other alternatives. Others who saw themselves as "critical scholars" were invested in criticising anything that the ANC did, while white academics (not all of them, obviously) continued to shape the post-apartheid agenda from their blinkered and privileged perspective. Probably, this is why we face the present "crisis" in higher education, because some black African scholars are products of white privilege and white hegemony. Hence, they may be excused if they do not see themselves as change agents or revolutionary actors who are supposed to radically transform South Africa.

I benefited from the tail-end of the above mentioned type of higher education, which was not poised to mainly discuss assignments and tests in class, or prepare students for examinations, important as these may be, but to create a pan-African citizen who was consciously aware of the material conditions of his or her continent, and who was astute enough to identify neo-colonial and neo-imperialistic agendas that were meant to take Africa backwards. Some of our lecturers were able to shape our minds and thinking in such a way that we were aware of our roles as students and possible future leaders, and that we had to be serious not only with our studies but with our personal lives as well. Some of them were able to radicalise us and engender in us a voracious appetite for reading different genres of books as well as for the acquisition of knowledge. Some of us read books beyond those prescribed by

   Surviving a University Department from Hell

our lecturers in their course outlines, especially revolutionary and Pan-Africanist texts.

Unfortunately, unlike academics, African politicians were not as astute, as they would be the first to succumb to the clientelistic trappings that were being entrenched by the agents of neo-colonialism. By the late 1960s and early 1970s, some malevolent leaders had assumed power, usually through illicit means such as a coup d'état and so forth. The first agenda item for such leaders was to decouple universities and then attempt to annihilate academics and intellectuals.

Nonetheless, the revolutionary and critical spirit that the early generation of African scholars and academics had cultivated in African universities survived this retrogressive period and I also benefited from it. Thus, we would devour progressive books such as Walter Rodney's *How Europe Underdeveloped Africa*, Frantz Fanon's *The Wretched of the Earth* and Eric William's *Capitalism and Slavery*, among many others. Marxist and neo-Marxist texts were next in line.

Also, one of the major benefits I derived from this period was being exposed to courses that synthesised a multiplicity of analytical lenses of the social sciences. I immensely enjoyed one course in my first year titled *Introduction to the Social Sciences (SS120)*. This course introduced students to the various disciplines of the social sciences. It not only provided a panoramic appraisal of social science courses, but enabled students to appreciate the different intellectual disciplines encompassing the broad field of the social sciences. It was a whole year course and, by the time a student had completed this course, he or she would be grounded in the basic tenets of all disciplines of the social sciences, ranging from *inter alia* economics, philosophy and development studies, to mass communication, sociology and political science. The student would have been "thoroughly cooked" as we would say and would not come out "half baked".

When I joined Wits in 1997, my HoD at the time emphatically told me that there were no two ways about it: when it came to academia, *you either publish or perish.* I heeded his advice and started teaching, researching and publishing. At the time, when Wits employed you as a lecturer you would be placed on a three-year probation and every year you would be assessed in order to monitor and track your progress, on the one hand (so that if you were facing any challenges, then remedial actions could be undertaken to help you meet your goals), or "offloaded" if you had performed dismally, on the other. The KPAs were teaching (linked to recurriculating and curriculum innovations), research and publications, and community engagement.

Since this job also entailed embarking on doctoral studies, progress in this area had to be assessed. I knew that I had to get stuck into the work and put my shoulder to the wheel, so to speak, because this was the nature of the job. My thinking is along the lines that one does not become a professional athlete and then start questioning why one should train every day. Also, one should not ask questions why one should train in hazardous conditions if one has chosen to become a military special forces officer. That was it.

After three years, when all the prerequisites were met, I was appointed on a permanent basis. I did not carry the HoD's bag to his car whenever he left the office or fight his perceived enemies on his behalf. I just did my job. That is what the merit system is all about and that is why I love and respect this system.

Nevertheless, there was something at Wits that lingered from South Africa's past at the time, and this was racism, white privilege and white hegemony. It was not uncommon for black African lecturers to be treated like students or for white students to openly challenge them, especially when the lecturers marked white students down due to shoddy performance. There was also the unwritten rule that when a course that had been taught by a white lecturer was taken over by a black African lecturer, then assertions would be made by the white sections of the university that "standards had fallen".

I found out that this distorted and racist mantra of "standards falling" whenever black African academics occupied positions of authority would be sounded across South Africa throughout the democratic dispensation, and at UCT it was quite strident. In my view, such thinking led a white academic to even write a book on the "falling standards" at UCT just because there was now black African agency at this institution, which had once been a white citadel, even in the democratic dispensation. Moreover, had it been a black African academic who had written such a book, he or she would have been hurled before a disciplinary hearing on charges of "bringing UCT into disrepute".

I would argue that if it were not for the *Rhodes Must Fall* student campaign, which began at UCT, and the *Fees Must Fall* student protest, which erupted at Wits and then spread across South Africa with a ferocity and intensity never seen before in post-apartheid South Africa, patriarchy, white privilege and white hegemony at UCT and other historically white universities (HWUs)[6] would have remained untouched, with

---

6   HWUs were established to exclusively provide higher education to whites, and they were split along the lines of English white liberal universities and universities solely for Afrikaners.

individuals produced by such a system working comfortably in their parochial and narrow-based educational spaces.

This is not coincidental as the history of UCT and HWUs are inextricably linked to colonialism and specifically settler colonialism and apartheid. Indeed, the origins of higher education in South Africa date back to 1829, with the establishment of the University of the Cape of Good Hope – present-day UCT – and the University of Stellenbosch, founded in 1874. These early institutions of higher learning were established primarily to prepare white males for further educational training abroad. They were modelled after British institutions; their students were white, and their academic staff came primarily from Britain and other European countries.[7] Therefore, the student protests not only disrupted patriarchy, white privilege and white hegemony for a short period, but also shook higher education to its core.

Academics had become very comfortable in these white spaces where black African students and even academics felt "invisible". The white academics and their non-white allies could peddle any colonial, apartheid and neo-colonial content and paradigms at will, without any serious challenge from black African academics, who are usually disunited and focussed on their own survival in such spaces.

The "Mamdani affair" at UCT remains a case in point. Indeed, March 2015 was a turning-point for UCT as students forced the hand of UCT management and in the process put some privileged and bigoted academics and executives on the defensive. This year signalled the arrival of a new, militant

---

7   Mabokela, R. O. (1997). The Evolution of Admissions and Retention Policies at an Historically White South African University. *The Journal of Negro Education*, 66(4), 423-433.

                                    Surviving a University Department from Hell

and uncompromising student populace, whose main objective seemed to revolve around the objective of overthrowing patriarchy, white privilege and white hegemony at UCT. The university erupted in waves of protest action, initially triggered by the continued presence on campus grounds of the statue of the arch agent of British imperialism and a key colonial architect, Cecil John Rhodes.

The students' displeasure over this statue on UCT grounds coalesced into what came to be known as the *Rhodes Must Fall* movement. Initially, the university authorities resisted the students' efforts to have the statue removed from UCT grounds. Eventually, the students prevailed, and the statue was removed from campus grounds (after the students had thrown human excrement and other objects at this statue).

No sooner had the *Rhodes Must Fall* protest dissipated than the *Fees Must Fall* demonstrations erupted across South African universities in October 2015. In this instance, students were united against the increase of tuition fees for the academic year of 2016. As the protests continued, demands were made for "free and decolonised" education. These protests continued until 2017, albeit in a muted form. However, since then sporadic protests have erupted at the beginning of almost every academic year.

It is interesting to note that after being thrown into a tailspin and literally caught unawares, many universities responded with a flurry of "decolonisation" commissions, research and various initiatives aimed at responding to the students' grievances. Strangely, such "decolonisation" research, commissions and so forth were again championed by white academics and their non-white cohorts (similar to the way the *ubuntu* discourse was culturally appropriated by the former).

The culture of appropriation is quite strong in South Africa, where white academics, intellectuals, businesspersons and others of influence in society provide narratives pertaining to black African people's cultures, values, struggles, triumphs, lamentations and all their experiences, willy-nilly, because they have the resources on the one hand, and on the other they feel that they have a right to speak on behalf of the "native" who is not only "inarticulate but does not know what he or she wants" in this world. So, black African people must have white spokespersons, who will be better placed to verbalise their issues on their behalf.

This white arrogance and highly patronising behaviour is reminiscent of the colonial days where both colonial authorities and missionaries hijacked all the human endeavours of African people. This situation has left many black Africans mere spectators in national affairs, with their voices being either sidelined or silenced by esoteric pontifications by the predominantly white media and white academia.

One of the key issues that the students had demanded was the *decolonisation of the curriculum,* which they felt did not resonate with their material and historical conditions. They found some content quite irrelevant, as it had heavy dosages of European scholars' warped perceptions about Africa and was in most cases bereft of African scholars' bodies of knowledge, solidly built in the post-colonial era.

I totally agreed with the students' diagnosis and response, and when I became an HoD I made it my mission to decolonise the curriculum of the department I was heading. Little did I know that the resistance and backlash would be so strong and would result in me stepping down from the position of HoD two and half years later. Nevertheless, the smug peddling of

                  Surviving a University Department from Hell

irrelevant neo-colonial content in spaces such as UCT is mind numbing and I encountered a lot of this in the department I was working in.

I talked about so-called standards earlier. When one looks at the leadership of universities in South Africa at the present time, it is a sad state of affairs indeed. On the one hand, it has gone to justify patriarchy, white privilege and white hegemony and has authenticated the racist and myopic notion that black Africans in South Africa (and perhaps all over the world) are not fit to lead institutions of higher learning. On the other, the foregoing is entwined, at the macro level, with the misguided and racist appraisal that the ANC has failed dismally to govern the country, with some delusional pundits even expressing the view that the apartheid National Party (NP) did wonderful things for South Africa in comparison to the ANC. Such bizarre sentiments have been provided by some sections of South Africa in their critique of the ANC government's self-inflicted wounds, which are, for example, typified by rolling mass blackouts euphemistically referred to as "loadshedding".

The racist sections, which had gone quiet over the years or had groaned during the presidency of Thabo Mbeki, were now having such a field day and making noises that suggested the idea that *black Africans cannot govern or even rule themselves.* Such notions also revolved around the misguided and racist appraisal that Africans "are like children who have to be chaperoned or led by the hand" to organise their lives. Left to their own devices, continues this racist fallacy, "Africans will implode or self-destruct". Thus, the clamour by some HW universities to always "monitor" black African managers or university leaders is not something out of the ordinary, but it is informed by this racist appraisal of reality. Equally, it also emboldens racists and other retrogressive actors to be defiant of black African leadership. That is why in such spaces some black African scholars have been told to go and pick up files or boxes or make tea by secretaries or junior administrators, who "mistook" them for cleaners and so forth.

Coming back to the dire state of university leadership across South Africa, there are ruptures at the biggest university in South Africa, the University of South Africa (UNISA). According to news reports, pressure is mounting on the UNISA principal and VC, who has been described as a disgrace, to resign and face charges of corruption. This comes following an independent investigation commissioned by Higher Education, Science and Innovation Minister, Dr. Blade Nzimande, and which was facilitated by Professor Themba Mosia.[8]

At the University of Pretoria (UP), there are also challenges. According to media reports, the VC left the university after having been cleared of a sexual harassment allegation, which was investigated by the organisation.[9] At UCT, black African and female leadership was haemorrhaged with the immediate

____

8   Sithole, S. (2023). *Unisa VC LenkaBula crisis hits business school*. Retrieved from https://www.google.co.za/ url?sa = i&rct = j&q=&esrc = s&source =web&cd=&ved=0CAIQw7AJahcKEwi4193wxvP_AhUAAAAAHQAAAAAQAg&url =https%3A%2F%2Fwww.iol.co.za%2Fthe-star%2Fnews%2Funisa-vc-lenkabula-crisis-hits-business-school-da6be2a1-8f59-4b48-a3ce-ebe9be8e6e01&psig= AOvVaw3cZYERe9naUc5tb3qyEE1Z&ust=1688508232733030&opi=89978449 As this book goes to press, UNISA is under administration as instructed by Dr. Nzimande.
9   Charles, M. (2023). *Vice-chancellor Kupe leaves University of Pretoria early, after delayed all-clear on sexual harassment*. Retrieved from https://www.news24.com/news24/southafrica/news/tawana-kupe-leaves-the-university-of-pretoria-early-after-a-delayed-all-clear-on-sexual-harassment-20230614

   Surviving a University Department from Hell

past VC, Deputy Council Chairperson and Council Chairperson all being forced out of their positions in quick succession. Even though there are challenges at the University of Stellenbosch, with its VC being accused of nepotism,[10] I wanted to cast light on black African leadership in this book.

Why does South Africa in general, and higher education in particular, find themselves in this untenable position? I would argue that the national liberation as well as the national question were not fully answered post-apartheid. There are just too many carry-overs from the past that continue to reinforce colonial patriarchy, white privilege and white hegemony. For instance, the country's landscape is littered with statues of mostly white males who participated in the oppression of indigenous peoples. This also goes for street and road names, buildings, towns, and other natural landscapes. Some of the colonialists who sought to exterminate indigenous people are still living today through their symbols.

Again, this deficit can be attributed to the negotiated settlement that entrenched certain aspects from the past in a new socio-political and economic dispensation via the *sunset clause*. Our children are learning Afrikaans in very expensive schools, without the country even taking a pause and reflecting on this paradox and on the many young people who lost their lives or were maimed for life by the apartheid security forces. These young people had defied the "almighty" apartheid state and refused to be taught in the language of the oppressor: Afrikaans. This was in 1976 during the Soweto Uprising.

---

10 Farber, T. (2023). *Nepotism claims against Stellenbosch University VC to be investigated.* Retrieved from https://www.businesslive.co.za/bd/ national/2023-04-18-nepotism-claims-against-stellenbosch-university-vc-to-be-investigated/

Almost thirty years into democracy, nothing has changed and, in fact, parents are willingly letting their children learn Afrikaans while paying exorbitant school fees in the process.

I have argued elsewhere that South Africa's transition to democracy is anything but normal. And yet, many sectors of society have sold the world on the "miracle" story of the "rainbow nation".[11] South Africa was not a normal society because it was underpinned and defined by the ideology of apartheid. Apartheid was declared a crime against humanity by the United Nations in 1974.[12] Apartheid was very intrusive as it defined the minutest of details of every person's life, including whom he or she could marry, where a person could reside or go to school and so on. In effect, South African society was heavily socially engineered. I have argued previously that South Africa must be socially re-engineered if it is to move forward, and if it is to erase all the remaining vestiges of colonialism and apartheid.[13]

---

11 Noyoo, N. (2019). *Social Policy in Post-Apartheid South Africa: Social Re-engineering for Inclusive Development* (1st ed.). Oxon: Routledge.

12 According to the United Nation's International Convention on the Suppression and Punishment of the Crime of Apartheid G.A. res. 3068 (XXVIII)), 28 U.N. GAOR Supp. (No. 30) at 75, U.N. Doc. A/9030 (1974), 1015 U.N.T.S. 243, entered into force July 18, 1976:
"The State Parties to the present Convention declare that apartheid is a crime against humanity and that inhuman acts resulting from the policies and practices of apartheid and similar policies and practices of racial segregation and discrimination, as defined in article II of the Convention, are crimes violating the principles of international law, in particular the purposes and principles of the Charter of the United Nations, and constituting a serious threat to international peace and security." Retrieved from https://www.un.org/en/genocideprevention/documents/atrocity-crimes/Doc.10_International%20Convention%20on%20the%20Suppression%20and%20Punishment%20of%20the%20Crime%20of%20Apartheid.pdf

13 See Noyoo (2019) above.

   Surviving a University Department from Hell

Many people died for South Africa's liberation. A lot of blood was spilt for South Africa's liberation, and freedom did not come easily. And it was not only South Africans who died for this country's freedom. A lot of citizens in most southern African countries, known then as the *front line states*, died for South Africa's freedom. And yet, when it comes to commemorating the country's freedom, this fact is treated as an inconvenient truth or a footnote of history that needs to be hidden away or even forgotten. After liberation, the situation was worsened when the black African leadership implored the country to "hold hands and sing Kumbaya" for the rainbow nation, while such processes like the Truth and Reconciliation Commission (TRC) were meant to serve as a vehicle for nation-building. Truthfully, the end result was that there were no consequences for the perpetrators of crimes against humanity.

I am reminded of the cold, heartless and calculated killers such as Eugene de Kock who headed the dreaded Vlakplaas and killed thousands of South Africans who opposed apartheid. This man, dubbed "prime evil", and his coterie of killers were so removed from their gruesome trade that they could be having a barbecue or braai and drinking alcohol while they were also decapitating and burning the bodies of their victims so that they would not be traced by their loved ones or comrades. Vlakplaas and other death squads did not end there, but pursued freedom fighters into neighbouring countries and killed citizens of those countries in the process.

I am reminded of the Matola raid in Mozambique in 1981 by these agents of death who killed many people. Then there was the Maseru raid in Lesotho in 1982 and Gaborone raid in Botswana in 1985. Also, the last incursion into Zambia in 1986 killed both South Africans and Zambians. Equally, Angolans and citizens of Eswatini suffered the wrath of the death squads and assassins. Since there were no consequences after the fall of apartheid for the many apartheid assassins or agents of death, such individuals retired peacefully and enjoyed their lives post their killing sprees.

Because there were no consequences, some sections of white South Africa became arrogant and even had amnesia by denying the existence of apartheid. Some of the apartheid denialists can be found in some political parties which are in opposition to the ANC's governance, on farms, and in civil society organisations, universities and so forth. Ironically, those who committed "crimes" while trying to liberate South Africa languished in jails and some continue to be incarcerated. It is mainly freedom fighters from the armed wing of the Pan Africanist Congress (PAC) Azania People's Liberation Army (APLA) who continue to wallow in prison. This is something that has puzzled me over the years and actually vexes me. While criminals have been pardoned, some APLA freedom fighters are still not free.

It is most puzzling that a cold and calculating killer, Janusz Waluś, who assassinated the iconic liberation struggle leader Chris Hani, was freed, and yet APLA combatants are still languishing in jail. What message does it send to the rest of the country and the world? This is what it means to be black African in post-apartheid South Africa, whereby those who were perpetrators of the worst and most gruesome acts against humanity have never accounted for their crimes and have been free to do as they please.

The above mentioned situation feeds into white arrogance and apartheid amnesia, and extends to universities as well. That is why some white academics continue to be insensitive

   Surviving a University Department from Hell

to the plight of black Africans and exhibit this high sense of entitlement that makes them think that they should always be in positions of power. I mean, what makes a person feel that he should be an HoD when he had engaged in arson and the smoking of drugs at the workplace? Conversely, why would an organisation's management and HR go out of its way to protect such a person while hounding the one who reported him? It is only because of white arrogance and apartheid amnesia.

Research by Gartushka (2009) argues that South Africa's post-apartheid era of democracy has required whites to renegotiate their identities within a new dispensation. Furthermore, the researcher observes that whites responded to this either through deep acceptance or strong resistance. For whites who resisted the new dispensation, the aim was to find ways of maintaining white privilege despite the end of apartheid. The research's analysis reveals the robustness of discursive attempts to block transformation within sites chosen for transformation. It also discovered that such discursive attempts were framed in ways that naturalised and normalised whiteness within the context of the new dispensation.[14]

I concur with the foregoing researcher's findings and note that whiteness has been normalised in some universities, to such an extent that even junior academics or administrative staff feel the need to instruct experienced black African academics. This feeds into the syndrome of "white is right" and that anything that is glamorous is supposed to be white or should be forced to be white.

---

14 Gartushka, I. (2009). *Discourse of whiteness in post-apartheid South Africa, as reflected in letters to the editor in the Cape Argus and Cape Times.* (Doctoral thesis). University of Cape Town.

This reminds of the advertising industry and its subtle agenda of entrenching white privilege and white hegemony. I have argued elsewhere that this industry is damaging the psyche, attitudes, psychology and mind-sets of South Africans. I can safely say that in the last twenty-nine years, almost all the adverts on television that depict, for example, positive living, good taste, glamour and so forth mostly feature white people, who act as customers, travellers and the like. And the location for such commercials is always exotic looking or European in appearance, such as the Western Cape, thanks to its Mediterranean climate. Should there be black Africans in such adverts where white people are promoting glamorous products, then they will surely play the stereotypical roles of maids, gardeners, petrol attendants and so on. If there are adverts that are mundane and promote less glamorous things such as cement, baked beans, curry powder and so forth, then it will definitely be black Africans playing parts in such commercials.

In the recent past, there was a controversy about an advert on black hair by one company dealing with hair products, which described African hair as dry, dull and damaged, while white hair was depicted as fine and flat. After there was a backlash, the company apologised to South Africans and discontinued the advert. However, this is not the first time that South Africa has had such a controversy related to racist and demeaning adverts. My view is that the advertising industry has been trying very hard to normalise whiteness in South Africa.

For the whites who deeply accepted the new dispensation in South Africa, their work, deeds and other contributions to South Africa's progress have been encouraging, sometimes even outstanding, in the last twenty-nine years. These white

                    Surviving a University Department from Hell

South Africans understand that they must add value to their country through their various works or endeavours. They go about their business doing good things, sometimes not even noticed for their efforts. These white South Africans are such a pleasure to work and interact with.

Unfortunately, it is the white South Africans resisting transformation who seem to dilute and corrode all the efforts being made by the progressive white South Africans. They occupy strategic positions in business and academia and are the ones who are spearheading a parochial type of politics in various opposition parties. These are the same white South Africans who go abroad and badmouth South Africa at every turn. And yet, it is the same country that has cushioned them and that gave them opportunities because of white privilege and white hegemony. These white South Africans have taken academia as the last frontier where patriarchy, white privilege and white hegemony must not be disturbed by radical social transformation. They are clinging onto a past that is in effect a relic and will soon be erased by radical social transformation, which is inevitable.

In the next section, I am going to substantively deal with my arrival and initial experiences at UCT. I highlight the grave anomalies I encountered, which set the stage for my eventual departure from this university. At the heart of my discussion is the shock and consternation I experienced after seeing deplorable activities unfold at a university that has been touted as "Number One" in Africa.

Chapter Two

ARRIVAL AND INITIAL SHOCK

I was lured to UCT by the allure of the university's status of being a premier university in Africa. I thought I would be engaged in ground breaking research and innovative academic activities there, as well as strategies pertaining to curriculum development and redesign. I thought that I was going to deepen my intellectual journey and engage in robust and informed debates with both academics and students. Also, I thought that the move to UCT would indeed serve as the pinnacle of my academic career.

I must confess, it was not easy to leave the University of Johannesburg (UJ), where I was treated with respect and dignity and, above all, appreciated at the faculty level. Also, what I liked about UJ was that one was rewarded for one's hard work. For instance, after undergoing a yearly evaluation with the HoD, if one had performed exceptionally well, one would receive a cash bonus on top of the thirteenth cheque. That was not all. If one published extensively, then one would be able to build a research kitty based solely on one's publications. So, one would not need to apply for funding from faculty, for example, because one would have accumulated funds from one's own publications. This is because each publication that an academic publishes, which meets the criteria proffered by the Department of Higher Education, Science and Innovation (DHEI), is subsidised and an amount is disbursed to the university.

At UJ, the DHEI subsidy, in the form of cash, is shared between an academic's department and him- or herself. This means that the more an academic publishes, the more he or she brings to his or her university DHEI funds as well as to his or her department and kitty. Then, if for instance academics intend to go to a conference, host a workshop or pay a research assistant, they do not need and go with a begging bowl to faculty to ask for money. The individuals will be able to engage in various academic and research activities because of extra funds at their disposal.

However, at UCT, no matter how much one publishes in peer reviewed and accredited works, no portion of the money accrues to oneself. One can work oneself into the ground and not be able to build a research kitty in the process. Then stragglers and those who do not want to publish are still able to access the money that other academics have worked hard for. Quite ironic, not so? Even if one has published, one will have to stand in a queue and beg for peanuts. That is why in my whole six years at UCT I only asked for research funding on one occasion. After that, I never bothered as it was pointless.

Apart from the foregoing issues, I found the conditions of service appallingly low for a so-called number one university. Academic salaries were a pittance in comparison to other universities of similar standing. Perhaps UCT management thought that the ocean and Table Mountain were also part of the conditions of service and that academics should be "grateful" for these things, which are non-essentials.

Despite these early disappointments, I thought the robust academic and high-quality intellectual engagements would make up for such shortfalls, even though it looked like the university seemed to be incentivising mediocrity at the expense of academic excellence. Why am I saying this? Well, in the department in which I found myself, there was palpable disdain for academic excellence, research, recurriculation and publishing. I found out that there were some lecturers who had not published in five years or even more, but prized themselves as "scholars". These lecturers never bothered to attend conferences, or even workshops for that matter. They would not even be caught at conferences organised by an association of schools of the core discipline which they taught in South Africa. While they were pouring cold scorn on research and publishing, they would be moaning how other disciplines were "encroaching" upon their "disciplinary turf" and publishing on issues that should be published by them.

I could not believe that this was happening in an academic department. When I asked a black African colleague – who was not only a serious academic but who was prolific in research, publishing and churning out postgraduate students – what was going on, he merely warned me to watch out for this group and to not share my research and publication outputs with them. I remember vividly his warning: "My brother, once they know that you are publishing, they will come after you!" He went on to say this: "Me, I keep my publications to myself."

This scholar was an expert in quantitative research and by my assessment he was a brilliant scholar. However, some individuals from the group of six lecturers (the Gang of Six) who would later hound me, were invested in making this academic's life at UCT a miserable one. He would resign in disgust the year after I arrived at UCT. After an announcement had been made in a staff meeting about his departure by the then HoD, the individual I consider an arsonist and drug addict said something to the effect of, "Good riddance... no one is indispensable". I was horrified! How could someone say something so mean? So callous? Luckily, the brilliant scholar was not at that meeting. I remember giving the arsonist and drug addict a cold stare. He and his cohorts could not be bothered and got on with the meeting after his comment. Anyhow, the brilliant scholar went on to do amazing things and continues to shine. To date, the department still does not have another expert in quantitative research.

I thought that I would be over my initial shock after arriving at UCT. However, there was more to come. As I was settling in, I found out that some courses were not only fragmented but frankly did not make any sense at all. For instance, I did not find a proper introductory course that introduced students to the discipline that was supposed to serve as a foundation course – the usual 101s or 100s as we would call them. Then there was the whole phenomenon of tailoring a course around a lecturer's deficits, or even whims for that matter. Because of this, it would be quite cumbersome to scaffold courses from the first year to the second year and then third and fourth.

For example, one lecturer who was and still is so obsessed with sexuality and his sexual orientation, would just turn core disciplinary courses into "sexiology". I wondered what some of the things he taught had to do with the core disciplinary content. Frankly, in my opinion, this individual taught students rubbish (my assessment was endorsed later by students, when they complained to me about being taught rubbish) and should not have been in academia in the first place. But he would be hailed as some "guru" by his admirers. I would soon discover that this individual and his friends did not have doctoral degrees (PhDs), but they were supervising PhD students. I could not believe what I was seeing.

In the same vein, he and his friends had been struggling to complete their PhDs and would always say that they were "busy", and that is why they could not complete their studies. Some of them offered a master's course that had six or seven students on a yearly basis, and it was touted as "the best in the country". Indeed, the same lecturers would be prancing up and down the department's corridors with a high sense of self-importance, the reason for which I could not fathom. As I write this book, only one of them has completed her PhD.

I would soon discover that, when it came to the allocation of postgraduate students for supervision, it became some "secret" affair, where those who were favoured would be given "bright" or "promising" students. Then those who were considered not worthy of favours were allocated "other" students. This is one of the first of many wrong things I changed when I became an HoD.

It was perplexing to find out that the same group of lecturers who came after me for no apparent reason – I will henceforth call them the Gang of Six – had the habit of marking students according to unknown or preconceived criteria: for instance, race, favouritism or something along these lines. Thus, the students they favoured were always given high marks.

I had heard some black African students grumbling in one of my classes that this was the standard practice in the department I was working in. It was difficult to pin down such malpractices when it came to assignments, but when I became HoD I found out that some of these lecturers would open the flap of the examination paper where the details of the students were (in order to see who the owner of the paper was, so that they could give him or her high marks) before verification of marks transpired, when the papers were brought to the HoD

	Surviving a University Department from Hell

and the administrative officer. Thereafter, the flaps would be opened to cross-check the identity of the student and the examination paper.

I was not only horrified but quite angry to find such malpractices being perpetrated by an academic (who happened to be white) in this day and age. After speaking sternly to the said individual and announcing to the rest of the staff that such practices would not be tolerated in the department, I reported the matter to the then acting dean, who happened to be white as well. Five years later, none of the lecturers who were involved in such malpractices have faced any consequences.

I now believed the black African students' grievances that racism was rife in the department and that some lecturers made sure that white students always got high marks, even if their work was shoddy. I had the evidence! This was not hearsay. That is why, when I become HoD, I made the department student-based and listened attentively to their voices, especially the voices of the black African students. Obviously, this was not welcomed by those students who served as certain lecturers' lackeys.

One thing was clear from the outset: I came with a different intellectual paradigm and tradition from what was obtaining in the said department. I called my classes students' "parliaments" or "assemblies" and pushed students to bring forth their intellectual and independent voices so that they could be heard in class debates.

I began to suspect that things were not right when, after posing a question, some students would ask how I would like it to be answered. At first, I was puzzled. Upon enquiry, I was informed by the students that some lecturers, whom they named, had the propensity to muzzle students with different opinions or views that did not resonate with those of their lecturers'. I was shocked.

How can a lecturer expect a university student to answer questions in a particular way or debate issues in a certain manner? And that the students' responses should please some lecturers or be in line with their thinking? What hogwash was this? Even at primary school level, my classmates and I were allowed to think freely, deeply and broadly. Now at university level this was happening – and at the "Number One" university in Africa to boot?

Before I could recover from this shock, I discovered that students were provided examination questions before final examinations in final or revision classes. These are important classes that all or most lecturers set aside to prepare the students for examinations. Usually, and which is standard practice, the students are provided the overall examination content, which is derived from what was taught to them in class, without going into specific questions. The students would be informed how an examination paper will be structured, for instance. For example, they would be informed that the examination paper would be split into two or three sections and that each question would be worth a particular mark. In such revisions, the students would be implored to read certain content and not limit themselves to class slides – another notorious practice I found at UCT. Students would even cite class notes of some lecturers, until I banned such practices in my classes.

Anyhow, while sitting in one revision class for one lecturer, I almost fell out of my chair when the lecturer started providing actual questions to the students. I was mortified! She stated clearly what the examination questions would be: "Section A, Question One is, blah blah..., Question Two is blah, blah...

     Surviving a University Department from Hell

and so on. Shocking! When I enquired of the few progressive colleagues in the department about this practice, they shrugged their shoulders in quite a resigned manner. After this episode, I knew that I had not only come to the wrong place, but that my stay would surely be unpleasant, unless I compromised on my values and principles. I had no more illusions about UCT after this shocking revelation.

Another issue I found strange when I arrived at the said department was a scholarship fund that had been donated to the department by the estate of a generous deceased benefactor. Worth a million Rand or more annually, monies would be disbursed to underprivileged students to help them top up on their scholarships – if there were shortfalls or something along these lines. To disburse such monies to students there would a meeting to determine who was eligible for such funding, with lecturers almost going for each other's throats. It was incredible. In such meetings there would be intense lobbying and jockeying, after previous weeks' deliberations on how such monies would be distributed to "deserving" students in a year. Some lecturers would be putting forward their favourite students and so on.

I asked the then HoD – after I'd attended one such meeting and after seeing my afternoon wasted when I could have spent it wisely writing a paper or researching – what the purpose of such a meeting was. Were there no better and more qualified individuals to do the work of vetting the students? I was given a vague answer, which was to the effect that the lecturers knew their students' needs best. I was not convinced. I nonetheless made a mental note and when I became an HoD I discontinued this practice. There was much blow back after this intervention and this issue was one of the Gang of Six's so-called grievances that led to me stepping down from the position of HoD.

In dealing with this scholarship saga, I presented the matter to the staff in a staff meeting. I noted that for an under performing department a lot of time was spent by academics on "vetting" students who were eligible for support. Surely, I reasoned, it would be preferable for them to use this time wisely to research, publish or recurriculate? I then tasked myself and the administration (admin) team to find out why the fund was placed at the departmental level instead of within a relevant structure at UCT. This is because I was not convinced by another unclear answer, which suggested that the fund had "always been in the department".

The admin staff and I secured meetings with specific officials in the offices that dealt with student finance. They welcomed us and were able to provide proper information on the scholarship and how it was bequeathed to the university and when. They also shed light on its intents and purposes. What they could not understand was how it had been spirited to the departmental level.

When I asked the finance officials if they could manage this fund at the central level, so that it could be taken away from the department, they noted that they handled millions' worth of trusts, scholarships and the like, and they also had clear and set criteria to determine eligibility. Managing one small scholarship would not be a problem to them. Moreover, the fund had been in their offices before. I then asked them if they would be willing to come and present what they had informed us of at a staff meeting, and they graciously agreed. I did this so that everyone knew what was happening. At this stage, I had also discovered how lies and "partial amnesia" defined departmental processes.

I had thought that people would be happy after the fund was returned to the central finance office. This was not the case, and this issue became a key "grievance" against me. I was dumbstruck at the time, but later the penny would drop, and quite loudly. It seems that the fund was used to "recruit" new students into the programme (this was the diplomatic version proffered by the institutional review process).

However, there was a much more sinister motive that compelled these academics to want to disburse this fund at the departmental level. I surmised later that this was to gain control over students so that the students could do the lecturers' bidding: "You see? I fought for you and secured funds for you so that you can complete your studies." Also, there was so much room for lecturers to dip their hands into the fund as it could not be determined if, after the needy student had received the money, a lecturer would not demand his or her cut. Due to this murky situation, a poor and hapless student could easily be hoodwinked and could be manipulated by an unscrupulous academic to even commit unspeakable acts for them. For example, I found out later that some students could be recruited and incited to go after certain academics whom the Gang of Six did not like. The Gang of Six was adept at this underhand and insidious tactic. In fact, the Gang of Six was very well-schooled in apartheid tactics of trying to destroy one's reputation, livelihood and life.

This practice by some academics to poke and embed themselves into the lives of students was quite rife in the department, with the Gang of Six leading the way. If it was not the scholarship, then it was giving certain favours to those they recruited into the schemes they had hatched for those they hated. Or they would "mother" students who were in effect young adults and had left their parents at home and did not need other "parents" in an academic department. I found this behaviour not only odd but felt that it debilitated and infantilised students.

But the one thing that topped all the malpractices in this department is what was called "counselling" services provided by one member of the Gang of Six. She prized herself as "caring" for the students' well-being "beyond the call of duty".

I first noticed this strange practice in the department when I found chairs lined up in the corridor next to the wall of her office, just like they are in waiting rooms in hospitals or psychiatric wards. At first, I thought students were consulting about the courses, lectures and so on. However, when I kept seeing so many students going into her office, I asked the then HoD what was going on. She answered, in a resigned manner (again!), that the said lecturer was "counselling" students and that she had warned her many times to stop this malpractice.

For those who do not know the intricacies related to professional degrees, the facts are that lecturers teaching them (I am speaking for the discipline that this department was offering) in South African universities must all be registered with a professional body. Otherwise, they would be committing a crime, as legislation clearly stipulates that those who teach future professionals should themselves be in good standing with the professional body. I had found out earlier that this rule was flouted in the department and some lecturers did not bother to register or update their professional status with the professional body. When I became HoD, I made sure that everyone who taught on the programmes was registered and that their professional standing was up to date. This again earned me the ire of some of the members of the Gang of Six.

   Surviving a University Department from Hell

To be fair, others from the Gang of Six were diligent about this issue.

Coming back to the "counselling" saga, it was shocking that not only did one lecturer see to it that she "counselled" students, but also invited her friend to offer "counselling" services and even demanded an office for her friend. When I refused, she went to the dean. This pattern would come to define the whole of my two-and half-year tenure as HoD. I will flesh this issue out more in the next chapter. Nevertheless, this malpractice was picked up by the deputy registrar and a query was sent to me, and I was asked about this serious anomaly and risk to the university. In my response to the deputy registrar, where I clarified matters and the steps I had taken to stop this malpractice, I also concurred with her. I then copied the dean, who had supported the individual who was providing "counselling" to students. This malpractice was only temporarily suspended when I was the HoD. When I stepped down, it was reactivated by an interim HoD who took over from me. I will discuss her tenure later.

It is important to note that there are risks involved when a lecturer chooses to counsel his or her students because he or she will have unfettered access to students' personal information and most intimate issues about them. This then allows the lecturer to have power over students and enables him or her to do as he or she pleases with the students. The second issue is that such behaviour is illegal, and the country's legislation is very clear on this. What is more irksome is that the university has established specialised psychosocial services to help students deal with their various psychosocial challenges. And yet, here was someone, running a counselling service when she should have been publishing, recurriculating and teaching relevant content. If you ask me, this is outright criminality and the said individual needs to account for the many young lives she has damaged over the years through her counselling services, while she was a lecturer all this time. From all accounts, I think she is still supported by the dean and continues offering her "counselling" services.

Having highlighted the above illegalities, let me drill down to the outright criminality and corruption that existed in the department and, from all accounts, still exists. This pertains to a provincial government-funded programme for capacity building in a particular subject matter or intervention. For several years, lecturers who were supposed to be involved in the training and capacity building of certain personnel at the provincial level were paying themselves "salaries" from this programme. Instead of paying only capacity that they had in-sourced to train on this programme, the Gang of Six and the former HoD I took over from paid each other "salaries" from this programme.

When I became HoD I was enticed into the scheme. I was told that I would receive R10 000 as "project leader", since I was the HoD. Immediately, I sensed that this was not right and there was something terribly wrong here. When I used to work in government, we used to call this "double dipping". In my view, the lecturers were supposed to have used their time on this project as part of their community engagement or social responsiveness. The rest of the in-sourced capacity should have been paid by the project. So, I refused to get a "salary" and I asked the senior administrator if this was normal. She answered that this anomaly had been going on for years. I then asked for a meeting with the provincial government officials to get to the bottom of this issue.

                              Surviving a University Department from Hell

When I met the officials from the government at the provincial level, we were on the same page. They agreed that this practice must be discontinued. We made this adjustment with the admin team soon after this meeting. There was an immediate uproar from the Gang of Six, with the drug addict and arsonist leading the charge against this decision. Immediately, this matter was "reported" to the dean. I was supposedly doing things any old how, and "abusing" my authority, among other cries.

A meeting was called by the dean to discuss my supposed "abuse of authority". This is another pattern that emerged during my tenure as HoD. Whenever the Gang of Six or any of their members was not happy with me, even if this issue was far-fetched, and it was reported to the dean, the dean would call me to her office as if I were an errant schoolboy being summoned by the headmaster. This bizarre type of interaction went on for some time until I told the dean on one occasion in her office that it would be the last time I would answer her "callouts" for something that these lecturers had reported to her and with which they, in effect, had nothing to do, as it did not fall under the purview of their KPAs. They should have stayed in their lane, as it was not their KPA.

In this encounter, she again reiterated her call and that of the Gang of Six for me to step down. She said she would recommend to the DVC (teaching and learning) for me to step down. I said to her, "Go ahead... do what you got to do". At this point in time, I was totally fed up with this dean's lack of professionalism and incompetence. She was clearly in over her head. I will unpack these matters in the next chapter. Nevertheless, I recused myself from this corrupt programme and refused to be associated with it. I informed the dean that she could oversee it with these corrupt lecturers, as far as I was concerned. Several months later, I got wind that payments had been discontinued after the dean had met the government officials herself. After this came to pass, the drug addict and arsonist came to my office and said, "So you feel vindicated?" I just glared at him.

Lastly, I want to highlight this department's semi-chaotic existence, where lies and feigning of amnesia defined processes. I came to find out that it suited some lecturers to be working in this kind of an environment. Why? Because it would be easy not to focus on the academic project and engage in so-called counselling services for students or paying themselves "salaries" from a government-sponsored programme in which they should have participated as part of their community engagement or social responsiveness.

For example, all staff meetings were recorded by longhand by a junior administrator and with no recorder. This meant that certain key decisions that were supposed to have been taken in a staff meeting could be easily challenged by a rogue staff member who wanted to wiggle out of certain responsibilities. This minute-taker's skills were not so flawless, to say the least. And I could not blame the admin person because the meetings were mostly raucous, with the Gang of Six trying to assert their position, no matter how ridiculous it was.

This pattern would continue when I became an HoD. However, I made sure that we recorded the meetings and bought a recorder for the admin staff. There was much noise and push back after I introduced a recorder. Some claimed that they did not want to be recorded, while others invoked the country's legislation, for example Protection of Personal Information Act. I reminded the Gang of Six that the staff meeting was not a personal space, but was for UCT. Everything discussed and

Surviving a University Department from Hell

deliberated in the staff meeting was about UCT matters and not staff members' personal issues. This space also fed into UCT policies, procedures and structures.

Another strange phenomenon that I could not fathom was when students submitted their assignments. Whenever this happened there would literally be a mob of students submitting their assignment to the junior admin officer, who was expected to stamp all the assignments and log them in as submitted. Many times, he was overwhelmed. Okay, let us forget about submitting assignments digitally (this was before the coronavirus – COVID-19 – pandemic), but surely there were better ways of doing this?

I raised this matter in a staff meeting, and no one seemed to offer anything meaningful. So, I met with my admin team and asked what the purpose of certain cupboards in the corridors was. Many of them were disused. The admin team came up with a brilliant idea and noted that the departmental handyman was also a skilled carpenter, and we could turn the cupboards into assignments boxes. We then procured the services of the handyman, who then turned the cupboards into assignment boxes. After this intervention, there were no more crowds of students in the department's corridors when it came to the submitting of assignments.

To my surprise, even something as mundane as this was not welcomed by the Gang of Six. They were not happy with this development. If something good was implemented in the department and it did not come from the Gang of Six, then it would not be supported, and they would fight it. This was what I experienced when I became an HoD.

Chapter Three

BECOMING AN HOD

When I was interviewed for the position of associate professor at UCT, I was in fact making a lateral move from my previous organisation and there was no promotion. This was after I had spent three years at UJ in the same position. I knew that I was losing out on my academic mileage as I had been about to submit my papers for promotion at UJ. However, the veneer of UCT and other personal considerations compelled me to move to UCT.

In part one of the interview (as it was split into two parts, with a latter section that entailed making a presentation to the staff and interview panel on a topic that was chosen by the department I had applied for a position in), the then dean, who is now heading another university, asked me if I would be willing to serve as an HoD and also wanted to find out how I was going to deal with conflict if I got the job. There was thus already an expectation that I would be an HoD, as the incumbent was about to retire. I answered in the usual classical way of bringing people to the party and endeavouring to find a common solution. Little did I know that I was headed to an extremely toxic and vile space.

What was clear though in the interview is that the university was well aware of this ramshackle department that had very few academic outputs. When I was eventually approached to be an HoD, I was not keen and declined the first and second time. I only agreed after the third approach. After studying it and its personnel for almost a year, I was not interested in being HoD of this department. I took meticulous notes in staff meetings and was able to decipher on my own that this department was fraudulent and operated like a ponzi scheme. How I wish I had stuck to my guns and not accepted the offer to head such a department from hell. However, that is water under the bridge now.

After it was announced by the dean (who came after the one who had gone off to head another institution and who led the deanery before the questionable deans discussed in this book) that I would be the next HoD, the disappointment from the Gang of Six was palpable as they'd wanted the drug addict and arsonist to be the HoD. That day, they all knocked off early (much earlier than their usual early time) and the department was quiet. This was before the drug addict and arsonist came to "congratulate" me. He asserted that he "played the ball and not the man" and I just shook his extended hand as I was not convinced by his hypocritical gesture. Next to follow was the white lecturer who turned all his courses into "sexiology". He pretended to congratulate me and noted that he "did not want any form of conflict". Later, this was proven to be a big lie.

The first order of business for me was to send an email to all staff to thank them for their support and to ask them to join me in forging a new agenda for the department. I then met each staff member in the department and had one-on-one conversations with them about almost everything pertaining to their career advancement and what they wanted to see happen in the department. I took down notes in every meeting. This was not my first rodeo, so to speak.

When we'd had our post examination meeting the previous year, I had stated to the staff that there was no one department or team. I thought this could be rectified by restarting all activities and seeking to forge one team in the department. I thus proposed that we go away for a three-day planning and team building session.

One thing I faced at the outset was the so-called lack of funds at faculty level. I wonder where the drug addict and arsonist is presently getting the money for his activities. I never received the support that this criminally-inclined individual receives from the university, including from the new interim vice chancellor. I will return to this issue soon. After managing to scrounge something from the then acting dean, I managed to take the staff on such a retreat.

What guided us at this session were the UCT strategic vision and the Institutional Review that had been conducted by UCT and which had found serious deficits in the department I was now heading. There were recommendations that were made by the Institutional Review and which the department had to implement. They ranged from the "trimming down" of some courses (as the department was heavy on teaching. Also, there was duplication of content, which needed to be streamlined), to boosting research and publication outputs. There were several challenges that had been identified by the Institutional Review and that the department had to address.

After studying the individuals in the department, I had no illusions that implementing these recommendations would be an easy task. However, I thought that there would be a common objective of responding to the Institutional Review, given the fact that the department had been identified as performing badly by an independent panel of experts. I thought everyone would come to the party, since it was a case of self-preservation. At the retreat, it became quite apparent that many were not prepared to take responsibility for the department's dismal

    Surviving a University Department from Hell

failure. Some pointed fingers at the former HoD and cast aspersions on her tenure. In the lead was the Gang of Six (as usual). At first, I was taken in by their theatrics of shedding tears after explaining how they had been "traumatised" by the former HoD – an accusation that would later be levelled at me. Indeed, these "Oscar winning performances" by the Gang of Six would characterise my HoD tenure.

In structuring the strategic planning retreat and team building, I invited officials from HR, the research unit of the university and deputy dean (staffing) to explain what the university required of the academics to get their careers moving forward. After these presentations from the UCT officials, there were question and answer sessions and clarifications. There were also the usual team building exercises.

With hindsight, I can now see that the Gang of Six had a long-term plan to disrupt my tenure at an opportune time and then overthrow me. It was clear that they were not really enthused but went through the motions of the strategic planning. However, I was very clear on what I thought the best course that the department had to take so as to become a première academic and research space, not only in South Africa but in Africa. That was my vision, which entailed, among other things, offering high quality postgraduate development courses anchored in African realities. That would have been the department's niche.

In quickly addressing the publication deficit, I proposed the notion of "low hanging fruits", whereby the best research reports and theses by postgraduate students would be turned into scientific scholarly papers. To do this, I proposed that weak and unpublished lecturers pair themselves with either me or another senior academic in the department, and then invite the students who had undertaken such research to be part of the teams.

"Brown bag" sessions were implemented, where we could discuss research issues or joint publications. In fact, this idea was advanced by several people in the department and not only me. Due to the so-called lack of funds, I used my own money for the drinks and eats for the first brown bag session. I remember vividly that when one of the Gang of Six was offered something to drink or eat by the senior admin officer, she just pushed them away with an expression of disgust on her face. That is how rude these individuals were, and yet I was being accused by the dean and faculty of being uncollegial. This was the first and last time there was a brown bag session because the next time I found myself sitting alone in the room we used for staff meetings. The resistance had begun. This was barely two months into my tenure.

I must mention a very important issue here. There was a group of serious, hard-working and well-intentioned colleagues who were supportive of the new initiatives that I was proposing and introducing, in line with the strategic vision of UCT, the higher education imperatives of the country and the National Development Plan (NDP) (2011). This group of serious academics and officials was always drowned by the noise and side-shows of the Gang of Six. They were never considered by the dean, DVC (teaching and learning) or other senior managers in the faculty, not even once, when they were supporting the spurious and malicious claims of the Gang of Six.

The department was effectively split almost in half. The senior admin officer, four academics and I were on one side, and the Gang of Six on the other. The junior admin officer was

   Surviving a University Department from Hell

split between the two groups. The Gang of Six somehow had a hold on him and he would do certain wrong things they asked of him. However, eventually he would report to me certain malpractices, after he got fed up with being used by the Gang of Six. I had warned him that such behaviour would result in him losing his job, while the Gang of Six would be secure in their jobs. Indeed, this came to pass.

All the senior managers at the faculty would go out of their way to support the Gang of Six, at the expense of the hard-working and focussed group. I had complained to the faculty senior managers and even the VC that this was not fair, where one belligerent and rogue group dictated terms in the department because they were supported by senior managers at faculty level. This bizarre behaviour of rewarding one highly toxic and non-performing group over those who were focussed on the academic project in the department made it feel like a form of cult or criminal cartel was in existence in the university. Those who belonged to this cult or cartel were rewarded handsomely, regardless, and fiercely protected by the powers that be. This strange situation continues to this day.

Nevertheless, during this period I can safely say that I was still coming out of a close to seven-year stint with government, having worked at the highest policy decision-making level as chief director/social policy specialist in the National Department of Social Development. This was prior to joining UJ. Some of the ground-breaking work we did with my colleagues in my unit and those from a department at the University of Oxford, was institutionalising evidence-based policy decision making and research in government, especially in the social cluster. My unit further extended this work into the Southern African Development Community (SADC), where we had successful Social Policy Round Tables and training sessions of senior civil servants and policy decision-makers from almost all SADC countries. These were convened in Livingstone, Zambia and Swakopmund, Namibia. I had operated at a regional and continental level, unlike some of the Gang of Six who have only worked in that dysfunctional department.

In fact, the lack of professionalism and maleficence in that department had always made me feel as if I had been working in a dysfunctional and corrupt municipality and not working at the "Number One" university in Africa or even working at a taxi rank.[15] Anyhow, I knew what needed to be done. I presented my vision to the staff, and no one objected to it. Also, we came up with a "charter" related to behaviour of conduct. The "dos and don'ts", as we called them. Everyone agreed to engage in proper communication, behaviour, transparency, and similar positive behaviour.

After the strategic planning session, I approached the then acting dean and proposed to devolve more power to staff by introducing a new position of deputy HoD. I then nominated none other than the drug addict and arsonist, who had been complaining of "marginalisation". Suffice it to say, this was the biggest mistake I made as an HoD. This individual would go to town to undermine me, stabbing me in the back at every turn. The situation became so untenable that I had to ask the acting dean to remove him. The fall-out was excruciating. I then nominated an academic from the serious group – a black African South African. We worked well until I stepped down, two and

---

15 In South Africa, minibus combies are also referred to as taxis. This sector is renowned for much bloodletting, where competition for routes often flares up in shoot-outs known as "taxi wars". This is an almost perennial phenomenon in South Africa.

     Surviving a University Department from Hell

half years later. He was supposed to have been the next HoD, but because of racism, corruption and other murky criteria, he was sidelined. I will cast light on this issue towards the end of this chapter.

One of the things I had promised students, especially those to whom I'd taught particular courses before I became HoD, was that I would make the department student-based if and when I became HoD. Before this even transpired, I had picked up on the students' complaint in my classes that there were no platforms to debate and present papers as students. They were very dispirited and complained that there was no intellectual engagement in their department. It was just lectures and that was all. And badly delivered lectures, for that matter, with no robust debates allowed in the classes. So, I said to the students, "Let us have a student dialogue". They thought that I was kidding. I went to the HoD to seek permission for a dialogue. Then I appointed them to run the show with me guiding them. I went and engaged the UCT media and presented my idea for the dialogue and they said that they would cover it.

After partnering with another organisation, a dialogue to discuss how young people could define an African vision and lead the march towards a better Africa was successfully convened.[16] My vision was to have an engaged student body that participated in matters of the department, so that we could identify and select the future leaders and lecturers from the group, for the department. I wanted to also create a student Volunteers' Corp. In line with this thinking, we (here

---

16 UCT (2017). *A civic mobilisation dialogue.* Retrieved from http://
   www.socialdevelopment.uct.ac.za/news/research-hub-launched-uct-
   department-social-development

I was working closely with the serious lecturers to whom the dean and other senior managers in the faculty never paid any attention) launched a Research Hub, which would act as an "incubation for research innovations in the Department of …" Furthermore, the hub's mission was captured accordingly: "This programme is meant to groom the next generation of academics and researchers, specifically those who come from previously disadvantaged groups. The programme offers internship, mentoring, teaching, research and administrative skills."[17]

My colleagues and I began to energise students in a sterile department that was already becoming moribund and redundant. One evening (almost like clockwork, most of the Gang of Six would on a daily basis waltz into the department around 9AM, and then proceed to drink coffee and smoke and gossip for another hour and then knock off early afternoon), one of the serious lecturers approached me and alerted me to a serious concern he had. I asked him what the matter was, and he informed me that he suspected that students rummaged through refuse bins and ate what they found there. I was not only horrified but confused as to why something of this nature could happen in post-apartheid South Africa and at the "Number One" university in South Africa.

To be sure, we set out to test my colleague's hypothesis by buying bread and peanut butter and leaving them near the refuse bin. Next morning, the bread and peanut butter were gone. We did this several times and the results were the same.

---

17 Department of Social Development (2018). *Research Hub Launched – UCT Department of Social Development.* Retrieved from http://www.socialdevelopment.uct.ac.za/news/research-hub-launched-uct-department-social-development

   Surviving a University Department from Hell

We then concluded that indeed there was serious hunger among the student populace. We were sure that it was students, as only a person with a UCT identification card could access the building. Also, my colleague had seen some students going to the corner where the refuse bins were. Several weeks after this, my colleague used his own money to buy more bread and peanut butter, and the results would be the same as in the first instance.

Then one day, early in the morning (we were usually the only two lecturers who arrived at the department between 6:30 and 7AM, like clockwork), we brainstormed about a food programme. Instead of just finding bread and peanut butter, why not turn this challenge into a pilot project and involve the students to find solutions to their own problems? We thus wrote a concept note for this initiative and made it a pilot project, which would run for six months. Fortuitously, there was a group of students who were already doing amazing work around campus. We thus asked them to bring their efforts "back home" to their department. When we tackled this challenge, we never envisaged the magnitude of food insecurity and hunger at UCT. In the concept note, we argued:

> *... Practitioners are trained to understand and address situations and forces that impact on people's well-being. Similarly, ... are trained to be dynamic professionals who are ready to promote social change and foster problem-solving, empowerment and the liberation of people to enhance their well-being. As such, they are expected to intervene at the points where people interact with their environments. Both the fields of ... and ... focus on enhancing people's well-being and the quality of life of individuals, families, groups,*

and communities. Students who acquire such critical tools of enhancing people's well-being and their quality of life constitute the cadre of students at the University of Cape Town (UCT) who are studying various degrees. These students come from different socio-economic backgrounds. It is important to note that many students at an affluent university such as UCT come from very poor backgrounds. A good number of these students face challenges of food insecurity and hunger as they strive to finish their studies. Students who are pursuing their studies in ... and ... also face similar challenges. For these students to concentrate in class, they must eat. Anecdotal evidence suggests that many students in the Department of ... experience food insecurity and hunger. Many have not had any recourse to food aid and thus come to class hungry. This is because not all students can afford a meal every day and lack of food makes it hard for them to be alert, concentrate in class and participate in all educational activities. It is due to this reason that the Department of ..., in collaboration with the ... – a non-profit organisation (NPO) – have founded the Department of ... Food Security Outreach Programme (FOSOP) to reduce food insecurity among the student population. FOSOP is running as a pilot programme within the ... Department until 31ˢᵗ December 2018.[18]

After gaining traction, the FOSOP became so popular that the university's top management took notice. Thereafter, the

---

18 Department of Social Development (2018). *Food Security Outreach Programme – Department of Social Development.* Retrieved from http://www.socialdevelopment.uct.ac.za/news/food-security-outreach-programmedepartment-social-development

     Surviving a University Department from Hell

university's management then approached us to explain to them how the FOSOP worked. When we met the top management or their representatives, we were informed that they desired to upscale the FOSOP and extend it to the rest of the university. Not only were we relieved that this issue would be tackled at the highest level of decision-making in the university, with more resources deployed to it, but we were also happy that the myth of "a happy" student populace had finally been debunked.

Through the FOSOP we were able to demonstrate to the university's management that the country's poverty and inequality were sharply etched into the social fabric of UCT. Thus, one part of the university was poor, hungry and underdeveloped while the other was rich, well-resourced and opulent. After this, we felt that our job was done.

After UCT management took over the FOSOP, the number of students who needed food swelled. According to UCT: "The UCT Food Security Programme, which was introduced last year, resumed on Monday 28 January 2019. The programme is a collaborative initiative between several departments, as well as student and staff volunteers from across the university."[19] Furthermore: "Currently, the Food Security Programme feeds 600 students every weekday on campus. Meals are pre-packed and delivered to UCT campuses by the Food Connect Service."[20]

---

19 UCT (2019). *UCT Food Programme.* Retrieved from https://www.news.uct.ac.za/article/-2019-02-01-uct-food-security-programme
20 UCT (2019). *Raising funds for campus food security.* Retrieved from https://www.news.uct.ac.za/article/-2019-06-14-raising-funds-for-campus-food-security

Students were innovative and had even managed to secure donations which buoyed up the FOSOP.[21]

When this initiative was unfolding, the Gang of Six was in the forefront, attacking it and making every effort to undermine it. Here we were, busy with the student volunteers going beyond the call of duty, to make sure that some students had food to eat so that they could concentrate on their studies, and then there was this group of rogue lecturers just bent on making sure that it never succeeded because they were not in the limelight. None of us had volunteered to work on the FOSOP for personal aggrandisement. This would be the pattern of behaviour throughout my two-and-a-half-year tenure as HoD, whereby the Gang of Six would undermine or disrupt any initiative that was not proposed by them. Moreover, they had nothing positive to propose, so they would engage in all manner of disruptive behaviour.

I have quoted the FOSOP at quite some length because the individual who offers "counselling services" made some disparaging remarks about this initiative in a staff meeting this year, 2023. From nowhere, the drug addict and arsonist had put this item on the staff meeting agenda. I wondered why this matter was being addressed in the staff meeting when the Gang of Six had fought against it. In fact, what was extremely annoying and irritating was that, after the said individual became HoD, he would copy and plagiarise everything that I had implemented and which the Gang of Six had opposed. Then, he would introduce them and pass them off as his. In one staff meeting,

---

21 UCT (2019). *Cool donation to student feeding programme*. Retrieved from https://www.news.uct.ac.za/article/-2019-03-08-cool-donation-to-student-feeding-programme

    Surviving a University Department from Hell

he introduced something along the lines of the research hub that the Gang of Six had fought against tooth and nail. In this meeting, some of the staff applauded such a "ground-breaking" initiative. Indeed, some could not help themselves and they clapped loudly in appreciation.

I would sit in these meetings and hear the drug addict and arsonist parrot my sentiments on decolonisation and the need for the department to research, when he had been the main culprit who had beat the biggest drum and opposed these initiatives when I had spearheaded them (including using a recorder in staff meetings). I was utterly nauseated. "What a fraud and liar," I thought to myself. Why did this individual and his cohorts fight me so much and at a very personal level? And yet here they were trying to play smart and not being clever, as the late Bob Marley had sung!

Anyhow, when the drug addict and arsonist asked about the food project, the "counsellor" blurted out, "I would not support it. It was a mess!" I could see her friends' faces and expressions of smug satisfaction. Days later, the minutes also reflected, I thought with some glee, that indeed the FOSOP was "a mess"! Well, if it was such a mess, why did the university top executive adopt it and expanded its reach to the rest of the university? Why did the university adopt such a mess? It was clear that now that they were "in charge", the Gang of Six was going out of its way to rubbish, pour cold water on or denigrate anything that I did or even achieved with my serious colleagues. They were busy creating a false narrative about the "mess" I supposedly left behind. That is why I was compelled to write this book. I was not going to allow this group of so-called academics to define me or control my narrative.

Another shocker came from the fourth-year students to whom I taught a policy course. As I taught and demanded rigour and incisive analysis from the students, some of them put up their hands and said that the issues I was "preaching" to them did not make sense. I was a bit confused and asked them if they thought that what I was teaching was useless. One of them, a black African female student, who seemed to have taken the leadership position on this matter, responded in this manner: "With due respect, we hear what you are saying about rigour and so on, and we have no problem with that. We have no problem with you and what you teach us. But we have a problem with some lecturers in our department who, frankly, teach us rubbish." Incidentally, I borrowed this phrase from this student when I reported earlier about a lecturer who turned courses into "sexiology".

I could see that this was something that had been burning in the students' minds for some time. Then several students voiced their concerns along the lines that they were not disrespecting my class but, because I always encouraged them to speak out, they felt compelled to do so in my class because, first, I was the HoD, and second, they were stifled by lecturers, whom they named and who belonged to the Gang of Six.

I moved from the front and sat behind a desk, just like a student, and let them air their grievances. After a while, I asked them what they proposed to do about the situation. While they were pondering on this, I suggested that we convene a student *indaba*.[22] The students were highly enthused and went about planning for the *indaba*. Then, out of the blue, some of the Gang of Six volunteered to convene the meeting together with the

---

22 In this case, it can be taken as a student dialogue.

     Surviving a University Department from Hell

students, after I had to attend a meeting in Pretoria. I knew that they wanted to intimidate the students and stop them from telling the truth. Thus, I alerted their leaders to write me a separate report.

True to form, one member of the Gang of Six wrote a one pager about the *indaba*, which was extremely shallow and deliberately so. I ignored and never bothered to engage with it. When I got a comprehensive report about the student *indaba* from the students, which highlighted major shortcomings in the department without naming and shaming lecturers, and which arrived at several recommendations, I was extremely impressed with their thoroughness and professionalism, unlike that of their lecturers. I submitted this report to the acting dean at the time. As usual, it was not taken into serious account because it exposed the Gang of Six.

I need to mention this disturbing issue before I proceed. Before I could settle into my role as HoD, I'd clashed with the previous HoD and we'd had a major fall-out. This was an individual whom I had revered and supported one hundred per cent when I came to the department and even before. It seemed that the HoD had no intention of retiring and she thought that she could control the department by remote, with me being her puppet on her strings. This, despite being at the department's helm for ten years. Ostensibly, she had supported me to become HoD with the misguided notion that she would control me.

Things became ugly when an HR person warned me that one portfolio, which had been created by the previous HoD, did not appear on the department's organogram. It smacked almost of a "super PA" (personal assistant) and money was being paid by the university to someone who did not appear on the department's organogram. The HR official rightly pointed out that this issue would come back to haunt me. If the former HoD wanted to continue paying the said individual, the HR official advised, then she should pay the salary from her research funds. The HR official noted that the post had to be de-established and asked for my opinion. I said that I concurred with her and said that the post should be de-established.

Already, the former HoD was grumbling in other circles that I was instituting "too many changes"; if it ain't broke, why fix it? This was her stance because she thought that there was nothing wrong with the department she had been heading for ten years. That was the first "grievance" I had faced, and it came from my predecessor. I was hauled before the then acting dean and accused of all sorts of things.

However, I had evidence to disprove the unfounded allegations. I was able to show the panel that had been constituted to investigate me that these changes were suggested by HR and that I had concurred with HR. Also, I informed the panel that it was illegal to create parallel structures to those on the department's and UCT's organogram.

After being interviewed separately by the panel, we came face to face with the previous HoD in a session with the then acting dean. In the last meeting with the acting dean and my predecessor, I expressed my disappointment in her and told her to her face. I told her that I had thought that she would use her emeritus status to mobilise funds for the department or engage in research and other academic endeavours that would propel the department to higher heights. But here she was, trying to run the department from retirement and stifling my vision and innovations. I was really disappointed with her. At that juncture, I had lost all my respect for her. Who did she think I was? I told the panel who interviewed me that I had never been anyone's lackey and would never be.

I was subsequently cleared of all charges. I learnt a valuable lesson from this first brush with lies, false accusations and innuendos. The department was a very dangerous place and one had to watch one's "six" so to speak. You could be labelled and accused of all sorts of unsavoury things. What helped me in this first tussle and others that followed was my penchant for attention to detail and keeping of records and evidence. That is what saved me and helped me to ride it out for two and a half years! If I had not had evidence, I would have been toast, as they say.

Anyhow, the Gang of Six, were to take something out of the previous HoD's play book and launched their own "grievances" against me three months later.

Three months after the débâcle with the previous HoD, the Gang of Six launched their own "grievances" against me and I had to defend myself against "bullying" allegations (when I was in fact the one who was being bullied by this group). This was because I had stopped them from double-dipping from the government-funded programme and the scholarship fund, and so forth. Based on such bogus claims, they argued, I had to immediately step down as HoD. Not because I was not performing; not because I had smoked drugs at the workplace; not because I had maliciously damaged public property; and not because I had engaged in arson.

According to senior managers at the faculty and the dean, these were such serious allegations that they warranted my removal from the HoD position. In my defence, one of the key issues I had raised was that the university was deliberately overlooking the other group of serious, hard-working and focussed lecturers and a senior administrator. I wondered why this was the case. To date, no one has answered this question. Why was this rabble-rousing and incompetent group, who did not publish, recurriculate or attend either local or international conferences, being given so much leeway to do as they pleased? It was as if these were members of a cult or criminal cartel, which the dean and the senior managers at the faculty level belonged to and which my diligent colleagues did not belong to, nor were even privy to. No matter how ridiculous their cries of wolf or claims were, the dean and senior managers at the faculty would close ranks around the Gang of Six and support them to the hilt.

This was an excruciatingly painful period as well as a corrosive one. Without any warning, some people have a supposed grievance against you, but have never approached you as the HoD to express any misgivings about your leadership. Everything was clandestinely done, as they had been mobilising for months, besmirching my name and reputation all over the university and even beyond the university. I was reliably told and warned by others in the department that they would meet in the office of the "counsellor" whenever I was attending a meeting out of town or a conference. The "counsellor" would even put her phone on speaker while they plotted how they were going to remove me. They even roped in the services of an HoD at another university who had an axe to grind with me.

At first, I had not paid full attention to the warnings because I wrongly thought that people would be busy focussing on the academic project. However, after I discovered how sinister the Gang of Six could be, I started paying close attention to such warnings from well-meaning colleagues, and also became wary

 Surviving a University Department from Hell

of this group. Thereafter, I became extra cautious. One thing I cannot understand to date is the ability of the Gang of Six to galvanise people at UCT to their "cause". Some people simply recruited themselves into the Gang of Six's feud with me.

Before I left UCT, I counted twenty-three individuals at this university (including the Gang of Six, minus those they recruited from outside UCT) who were invested in destroying me.

I do not know what these people's problem was with me as I did not work in the same department as theirs or even know some of them. That is why I would be quite perturbed when I would walk into a meeting and be greeted by a frosty reception or outright hostility. Sometimes, when I would be walking down the corridors of UCT, I would be surprised to cross paths with someone who would immediately take a hostile posture and start stomping past me while clearly being hot under the collar. On such occasions, I would look at the individual and mentally ask myself, "And now? What is this?"

I wonder why some people recruited themselves to be part of this evil fight waged by the Gang of Six against me. What did I do that was so wrong that I found myself being pursued by so many people at UCT, when I was actually doing my job? Furthermore, I still want to know what wrong I did to the Gang of Six for them to have been so invested in trying to basically destroy me. It is clear that their unsavoury actions against me were extremely personal. This was not about work; it was about annihilating Ndangwa Noyoo!

Some of the things I encountered during these five and a half years of torture were quite scary and damaging. I thus engaged the services of private investigators to smoke out the perpetrators of some of the evil and vile acts against me. I will not go into much detail here, as these issues are still being investigated.

The so-called grievances against me were not only spurious but mischievous and should not have been entertained by senior managers at the faculty and the acting dean at the time. However, it had become abundantly clear to me and to some of the hard-working colleagues who just wanted to focus on their work, that the Gang of Six was being backed by senior managers in the faculty and the then acting dean. When the acting dean was replaced by a new dean, the relationship between the faculty and the Gang of Six would be solidified and taken to higher heights.

The grievance process did not yield the results that the Gang of Six wanted: my stepping down or being removed from the headship. Since there was actually nothing that I had done wrong to this group of lecturers, apart from reminding them to meet their key performance indicators (KPIs), those in management who supported this group tried to let this group save face by coming up with some mediation type of arrangement. Meanwhile, the person who chaired the grievance process would become the next dean, who was heavily embedded with the Gang of Six.

At this point in time, I erroneously believed that there was due process at UCT, and justice would be attained at the end of the day. I would later discover, especially after the chair of the grievance process became the dean, that these were rigged processes and they were merely meant to hoodwink people into believing that "something was being done". In fact, when I tried to rein in the Gang of Six and failed, and reported this to the dean, she would constitute sham committees that would be headed

   Surviving a University Department from Hell

by particular "enforcers" at the faculty level. These phoney committees had pre-determined decisions, which would be in favour of the Gang of Six. It was these so-called committees that would turn out to be kangaroo courts after their initial purpose was supposed to make the Gang of Six adhere to the tenets of academia. Out of the blue, the "committees" would make a violent about-turn and suddenly be solely focussed on the HoD and his so-called lack of "collegiality".

In one of these kangaroo courts, which was headed by one of the dean's enforcers (one of the group I now called the "usual suspects"), a deputy dean, I found her and the committee she was heading extremely biased. This led me and the then deputy HoD in the department I was working in to complain to the then VC that the sham process was again authenticating the hateful and myopic position of the Gang of Six, among other things. Instead of looking into rectifying the Gang of Six's lack of performance and intransigence, it was shoring up these individuals' diabolical and ill-conceived motives. We noted that every time there was a fake process that was constituted by the dean, it always sought to undermine the HoD and sneak in the "step down" agenda, even if the Gang of Six was in the wrong. Also, the sentiments, views or voices of the other academics and officials in the mentioned department were totally disregarded by the dean and her "enforcers".

This deputy dean, during the above mentioned bogus process, observed that, even if one of the Gang of Six had said that they "had seen a pink pig walking up the stairs and it had shat on the stairs", she had an obligation to investigate the matter. This was a so-called senior manager, a deputy dean for that matter, verbalising such drivel. This white lady made this bizarre assertion after I had complained that the Gang of Six should not be throwing around accusations of trauma or being traumatised by the HoD, when in fact it was the HoD who was traumatised by this group and their supporters.

It was quite ironic that, after I had sought the dean's intervention to reprimand the Gang of Six for their refusal to implement the recommendations of the Institutional Review, she turned my request against me and used it to again advance the campaign to remove me from the position of HoD. The deputy HoD and I knew what the dean was trying to do. She wrongly thought that she was dealing with children. Therefore, the deputy HoD and I decided to approach the then VC, as I mentioned earlier, and wrote this letter to her after witnessing outright bias during the first sessions of the said sham committee:

Attention: The Vice Chancellor Professor...
8/11/2019

Re: Deplorable state of affairs in the Department of ...

We wish to bring to your attention that, whilst we appreciate and will participate in the dean's task team to support our department ..., we believe the problems in our department need a much more holistic and in-depth investigation. Hence, we have decided to write directly to you as the vice chancellor of this university. The malaise in the Department of ... has been in existence for a number of years. This is an untenable situation which we inherited. This high level of dysfunctionality and toxicity has in the main been exacerbated by a group of staff members who have consistently undermined and resisted transformation as well as efforts aimed at fostering a working environment that is based on mutual

    Surviving a University Department from Hell

respect and collegiality and raising academic standards in the department.

Perhaps these corrosive patterns of human interaction remain entrenched because it seems they were nurtured and nourished for a long time in our department. It is perplexing that this dreadful environment was left to fester for years without any intervention from higher structures of the university. For such a small department, it is equally disquieting that certain personalities have been left to hold it to ransom – by a group of individuals who want to only do things if they are in line with their own personal agendas and not those of the department and the university.

We write this letter with much misgiving and a high sense of hopelessness because we feel that there has not been any support for us to execute our leadership roles and responsibilities, especially when it comes to managing staff who totally disregard university procedures, policies and protocols, and who do not seem to understand what their core functions as academics are. Indeed, whenever there has been anything forthcoming from the aforementioned structures, they have always resembled a fault-finding mission, targeting the leadership, and not invested in efforts aimed at ascertaining why some staff members are, for most of the time, engaged in activities that are not remotely related to academia.

We also feel that this same group of individuals has been the one that has been given so much audience, by the same structures, time after time, while the department's leadership and the few staff members who seek academic excellence are simply ignored. We find ourselves in an unenviable situation where some academics hold the department to ransom and where we cannot execute the strategic mandate of the department, as they feign victimisation at every turn when they are asked to perform the duties requisite of any academic. Their consistent and strident demand has been that the Head of Department should step down due to their profound hatred for him and not due to gross misconduct that warrants a disciplinary hearing. This stance has not changed in the one year since the former HoD retired (notwithstanding the fact that she still wants to determine the strategic thrust of the department).

Thus, their demands culminated in a grievance process that was found wanting. Their allegations were tested through a rigorous process, and they did not stand the test. Flowing from the said process, recommendations were made, which the HoD adhered to, to the letter, while the same group has blatantly disregarded them. In the same vein, this group has not wanted any harmony in the department and has continuously gone on a smear campaign against the HoD across the university, in various structures, and while engaged in highly disruptive behaviour that has at times plunged the department into a state of semi paralysis. This has served to reinforce their agenda, which seems to cast the leadership of the department in a very bad light and to "prove" that there is "no leadership" in the department. Some of their actions have bordered on outright sabotage.

Being black academics, we are mindful of a corollary to this insidious agenda, which partly rests on the notion that black academics are incapable of playing any leadership roles. Furthermore, they continue to teach outmoded course content while always trying to peddle the notion that ... academics should be given special dispensation so that they can just teach and not be engaged in research and other scholarly endeavours. They also publicly declare in staff meetings that they will not publish and will not go to conferences – even when an international conference is literally brought to their doorstep, so to speak.

Vice Chancellor, we are not beholden to these positions. However, we take them very seriously and fully recognise that we not only have a responsibility to the university executive, council, and your office, but to the people of this land and the government. Also, due to principle, one cannot simply step down because a group of academics is hounding one from one's position. Indeed, when the department's academic outputs are scrutinised, the evidence will clearly show that most of the members of the same group of academics have not published or presented at an international conference for over five years.

We continue to work in this toxic and debilitating environment, where those who seek academic excellence are targeted by the same group. In this department, it is anathema to announce that a staff member has published. Research and publications are treated with disdain in this department and other yardsticks are being forcibly advanced to represent academic excellence. We have tried hard to move the department from academic oblivion to excellence by shifting it onto an axis of evidence-based research endeavours, publication throughput and academic citizenship. We have also tried to align this department to UCT's vision of an inclusive, engaged and research-intensive African university. However, the push-back has been very strong and we are left with no choice but to approach your high office to deal with this department's malaise.

Given the aforementioned culture, which continues to debilitate the academic mission of this department and which promotes non-core academic activities, we are praying to your high office to intervene in this department. We are thus calling for a deep diagnostic process that is evidence-based and evidence-

informed to root out the cited ills. All the issues we have raised can be substantiated through evidence. We are not moving from the premise of hearsay. In writing this letter, we are also acutely cognisant of the fact that this department is located in a premier university and should be at the forefront of cutting-edge research in ... issues, which should proffer solutions to the country's triple challenges of unemployment, poverty and inequality.

We have tried to move in this direction, by endeavouring to establish a research hub in the department with high-level meetings held with senior government officials from ... and .... and international partners, taking place. Our international partners have even pledged to secure funding for the said endeavour. However, we are hamstrung by the same individuals who just do not want to see any progress in this department. We humbly request your intervention in this matter.

Sincerely,

Ndangwa Noyoo (Head of Department)
.... (Deputy Head of Department)

Despite our valiant efforts and hopes, we did not get any support from the then VC. To this end, the freak show that was created by the Gang of Six and their enablers continued for two and a half years. The more I stayed on as HoD and did wonderful things with the group of serious-minded academics, the more the taunts, provocations, innuendos, incitement of students, lies and outright sabotage of departmental activities became pronounced.

After the Gang of Six had strongly expressed the view that it was either their way or the highway, I left them alone and worked closely with the hard-working academics and the serious official in the department. But they would just not leave us alone and continued with their destructive and disruptive behaviour. For instance, they weaponised the internal email communication system. When things would be quiet in the department, there would be a random and unsolicited email sent by one from the Gang of Six. "Dear All," the communication would go, "I presented a paper at a secondary school on topic x or wrote something in a newsletter for a non-governmental organisation (NGO) or I got an email from a former student who thanked me for my lecturing abilities" and so on. Then the responses would come fast and furious from the Gang of Six: "Wow!", "Well done!", "This is fantastic!" and so forth.

Such congratulatory messages would not be extended to the hard-working academics when they published in international peer-reviewed journals (and not an NGO newsletter) or presented at international conferences (and not to high school kids). Sometimes, the underlying message of such communication was about how publishing was not the "only important thing" in academia. I would know that such taunts and provocations were aimed at me. I would let them continue with their taunts via the internal email system.

However, I would also get fed up, at some point, and be irritated by these random, irrelevant and provocative emails. Then I would call the Gang of Six to order and remind them that as academics they could not be disparaging publishing. Immediately this happened, my email would be rushed to HR and the dean. The dean would immediately admonish me: "I thought we had agreed that the internal email system would only be used for departmental matters?" She would not even bother to follow the thread of the communication.

Other deviant acts pertained to outright sabotage of the department and making it ungovernable. For example, when we sought to host an international conference at UCT, the Gang of Six tried to make sure that it failed. By this time, I knew what kind of characters I was dealing with. To circumvent their nefarious agenda, I created various committees and leaned heavily on my student volunteer corps. These students did some extraordinary work. I also worked closely with the serious academics and the department's senior administrator. Despite fighting tooth and nail to derail the international conference, it took place, and it was a resounding success. This was the first time in the department's history that an international conference of this magnitude had been hosted at UCT. Predictably, most of the Gang of Six boycotted the conference (as if it were my career they were hurting). Two members of the Gang of Six participated in the conference and even presented papers.

As the conference was gaining momentum, the Gang of Six decided to have its own "conference". Suffice it to say, not only did it not generate any interest beyond the Gang of Six and their associates in the Western Cape, but it was a total joke and a flop. But the "counsellor" would declare it a "total success" in a staff meeting. When I decided to report to the dean about the Gang of Six's boycott, she did not even bother to respond to my text. That is the day I deleted her phone number from my phone and concluded that this individual was useless. There was no other way to describe her.

As regards those who participated in the conference, an edited book,[23] which had all their chapters and those from

____

23 For more information, please follow this link: https://link.springer.
  com/book/10.1007/978-3-030-50139-6

     Surviving a University Department from Hell

academics from other universities, was published. This publication was part of the "low hanging fruit" agenda I had explained to the staff when I had presented my vision to them, just after I was appointed HoD. I had pointed out to them that if we hosted an international conference, not only would they be able to present their papers at home, but they would be able to turn them into publications. This strategy seemed to fly over the heads of the Gang of Six.

Furthermore, making the department ungovernable was exemplified by a solidified stance of intransigence by the Gang of Six. Whatever was proposed by the HoD, the Gang of Six would refuse and then the dean would endorse their ridiculous position. For instance, the university had instituted an Institutional Review which had required the department to come up with an improvement plan. For example, some irrelevant and duplicated course content had to be weeded out from the department's curriculum, while some courses had to be realigned altogether. In regard to publishing, the department needed to publish.

Some of us who were not part of the Gang of Six took these issues very seriously and started focussing on increasing our publication outputs. This did not sit well with the Gang of Six. In one raucous staff meeting, the "counsellor" declared to me and everyone: "I will not publish or go to conferences!" She stared at me while daring me as she crossed her arms over her bosom. I asked her if she would not budge. She answered: "I will not budge!" Then one from the Gang of Six, who was always loud and made a noise in the corridors, added to the confusion. At that very moment I felt sorry for this woman. Really? It was not my career she was destroying. It was her career, not mine! But since individuals were able to not publish for more than five years and still be protected by a dean and senior managers at faculty level, I was no longer shocked or surprised.

However, I felt sorry for the students. Who did this person think she was, I thought to myself, to stand in front of students and teach them? Teach them what? If you do not research and publish, what can you teach students? This was criminal, I thought. Here was someone declaring that she would not publish or go to conferences while being employed at the "Number One" university in Africa? And yet when I was in the Democratic Republic of the Congo (DRC) in 2008, I'd found colleagues at the University of Kinshasa seriously mapping out a publishing agenda for their department. They had even launched an international peer reviewed journal! They were doing all this wonderful work in the middle of a civil war! The Congolese colleagues were extremely serious about publishing. And here I was at the "Number One" university in Africa, with so many resources at its disposal, but surrounded by some people who disparaged publishing!

I would like to ask the reader to put himself or herself in my shoes. What would you do?

Nevertheless, the Gang of Six had extended their disruptive behaviour to staff meetings, probably because they found them to be a soft target. When they came to a staff meeting, it was clear to see that they had met before and agreed on a particular course of action to either derail the meeting or insert their own agenda into it. These individuals spent so much of the university's resources plotting to oust an HoD or trying to destroy his career. If they had invested such time and energies into writing book chapters or academic journals, probably their publications would have increased.

I thought that I had seen it all. However, one staff meeting reached the lowest of levels when one female staff member, who was the anchor of the Gang of Six, literally insulted me. In early 2019, I had decided to go overseas for a month to engage in research and publish with my colleagues in Europe. I was feeling redundant at this stage, as there was no intellectual stimulation in my deplorable department. Thus, I took contact leave and made sure that I would come back before the academic year had unfolded in earnest. The Deputy HoD took the reins of the department. This was a cue for the Gang of Six to go to town and just wreak havoc while I was away and try as much as possible to oust me.

At this stage, I had made up my mind that my academic outputs would not suffer because of these individuals and that I would not allow myself to stoop to their myopic and non-performing levels. After I returned, and at the first staff meeting I had chaired, I queried certain things that had been reported by two members of the Gang of Six and that were inaccurate. Another issue that transpired was that they raised certain falsities in my name, while I was on contact leave. I asked them to explain why they had done so when we had arrived at a policy decision in the department that if there were certain misgivings about an individual that needed to be reported in a staff meeting, the individual in question should be there to answer for him- or herself.

Before I could get any answer from the two lecturers, the woman who was their co-leader (the drug addict and arsonist was the ring leader) stood up and aggressively walked to where I was sitting while chairing the meeting and shrieked at the top of her voice, while foaming at the mouth: "You think you have power because you are HoD? Why are you attacking so and so?" She literally stood over me while she wagged her finger at me and continued to shriek. Strangely, I calmly looked at this woman exhibiting the most uncouth and unprofessional behaviour I had ever encountered at the workplace. The reader must be reminded here that I had not talked to this individual in the first instance. I had not provoked her or even remotely addressed her in the staff meeting. The two lecturers whom she was supposedly defending against my so-called excesses were adults, who had their own mouths and voices and could have easily explained why they had followed such a course of action.

While this spectacle was unfolding, the Gang of Six members were impressed and the drug addict and arsonist, and the one who spoke on top of her voice in the department's corridors, made so much noise, stating that they would not "be comfortable" to have the minutes discussed because two of their members had been cited as breaching departmental policy. From the corner of my eye, I caught a glimpse of some members of the Gang of Six's expressions of smug satisfaction. They also seemed to be extremely impressed with the display of such uncouth and vile behaviour.

On the other side, I saw some of the serious lecturers' expressions: most of them were mortified. The co-anchor of the Gang of Six, before she stomped off and out of the staff meeting, sucked her teeth[24] and made a long sucking sound at me. Thereafter, she shouted on top of her voice, "Bullshit!" as she was busy walking towards the door.

---

24 In African and even black culture (as the African diaspora carried some traits from Africa to the Caribbean and the United States), sucking of one's teeth signifies, among others, utmost disgust, total disdain, disrespect or belittling of the other person it is aimed at.

   Surviving a University Department from Hell

I looked at the other staff members and asked: "Is this where things have come to?" Then I looked at the two members from the Gang of Six who were making a noise and told them to leave the staff meeting if they so wished. A week later, when I had reported this incident to the dean and HR, I was simply ignored. Later, when I had lodged grievances against the dean, the former DVC (teaching and learning) who had chaired this grievance asked me a silly question related to this incident. My main grievance against this dean was that she never supported me in any way and took the side of the Gang of Six at every turn. I will return to this issue shortly. Anyhow, the DVC had asked me to define what an insult was when I had pointed out that the co-anchor of the Gang of Six had insulted me in a staff meeting. Now, it is important to point out that when I had chaired this staff meeting and others, I had not done this on behalf of myself or family, but on behalf of UCT. We were discussing UCT matters and not personal issues. That space, the agenda items and everything we did in that meeting were supposed to be for UCT, and not for our own personal benefit.

At this point in time, I had reached low and bizarre levels of interaction with the dean. Whenever the Gang of Six refused to basically do their work or implement the Institutional Review, she would constitute some panel or ask another HoD (usually an older white man) to come to chair a session I should have chaired, which was supposed to have focussed on implementing the Institutional Review. On all such occasions, when the Gang of Six had exhibited rogue behaviour, the Dean had not reprimanded any of them. Not even once! While, on the other hand, I was being summoned at every turn and admonished by this individual who was supposed to support me.

Then it dawned on me that they had set out to make my tenure a failure. They were hell-bent on making sure that I failed as an HoD and could thus be relegated to the dustbins of academia. Then, when their scheme was failing, they could not contain their frustration and ended up shouting "bullshit!" in a staff meeting. By the way, this individual is a lecturer who would give her master's students distinctions in order to ingratiate herself with them. I had reported this behaviour to the dean, but she did not even bother to follow it up. Where in the world can a whole class of postgraduate students get distinctions? Can someone please tell me?

Also, it became very clear that the dean and the former DVC were in cahoots during one zoom meeting (we were now in the Coronavirus [COVID-19] pandemic and the freak show had gathered momentum), when we were again supposed to implement the Institutional Review. After the former DVC explained the purpose of the meeting and went through the motions of doing so, the discussion veered again towards the "step down agenda". First, as usual, it was the drug addict and arsonist who posed this question: "When is he going? June or July?... so that we can start afresh". This was in May 2020, and I was being squeezed by the dean and the former DVC into a corner, in order to make way for the Gang of Six's elevation. Then the "counsellor" asked what would be done to me after a grievance letter that I had written to the former VC had been leaked to the media.[25]

At the time, when a reporter had contacted me for a comment regarding the letter to the VC, which had reported

____

25 For more information, follow this link: https://www.news24.com/citypress/news/uct-academics-at-war-20200324

    Surviving a University Department from Hell

a "war" between the dean and me, I was so fed up with this group of UCT torturers that I chose not to be anonymous and just "let it rip", as they would say. This was the loophole they had been waiting for, to bring disciplinary charges against me. The former DVC (teaching and learning) said something in the zoom meeting to the effect that it was already being looked into. When the one who shouted in corridors saw that I was not going to be removed from the position of HoD right there and then, she could not help herself and blurted out loudly, "But we were promised!" Those of us who had suspected this conspiracy got the confirmation we needed! The dean, the former DVC (teaching and learning) and senior faculty officials (deputy deans and others) constantly met with this Gang of Six and indeed did plot to oust me several times. Lo and behold, as the drug addict and arsonist had predicted, in June 2020 disciplinary charges were levelled against me.

Before I delve into the disciplinary charges, I want to illustrate how the Gang of Six, HR and senior faculty officials would gang up against me after they had plotted somewhere. One day, and literally out of the blue, when we were about to embark on final examinations, after tabulating the continuous assessment marks, a call came from one of the dean's "enforcers", another deputy dean (the usual suspects, who were actually her friends) for the staff to meet downstairs in the room where we held our staff meetings. The then acting dean, the "enforcer" and an HR official, as well as the Gang of Six, were in the lead. I did not know what was going on but went to the room together with the hard-working colleagues. When we were all seated and the meeting started, it was evident that there was no clearly urgent matter to be addressed. They had gone and plotted elsewhere and wanted to ambush me into stepping down.

The "enforcer" began with a tirade about how things were bad in the department, while the serious and hard-working academics were bewildered as to what was happening. Then the drug addict and arsonist (as usual) began to move a motion that there was a need to have some caretaker HoD "so that we can start afresh". Then, when the one who shouted or spoke loudly in corridors was about to second this "motion" (it was clear to see how well and diabolically orchestrated this thing was), the most senior academic in the department, a white man who was about to retire, just called the deputy dean by his first name and told him not use apartheid tactics to hound an HoD. I will never forget that day. The senior colleague just tore into this deputy dean!

I had always respected this gentleman, who equally always respected and treated me well. He was and continues to be a very genuine human being: if he did not like something or what someone was doing, he would tell the person how he felt.

After this intervention by the white senior academic, other senior scholars from the other group expressed their disquiet and noted that they felt ambushed. Then, I asked the deputy dean what was so existentially threatening to the department that we had to be hastily brought to this meeting when we were busy preparing for examinations? When the drug addict and arsonist said something to the effect that they were being persecuted or something along those lines, I retorted: "On sabbatical?" When he was supposedly on sabbatical he was at the department, every day, fighting me.

After this resistance from the serious academics, the meeting was hastily adjourned by the dean's "enforcer". When this group

Surviving a University Department from Hell

saw that they were unable to launch their coup d'état, they all trooped out of the venue. After this highly unsettling encounter, those of us who were not part of this conspiracy were left quite miffed and puzzled.

As I pointed out earlier, the Gang of Six was adept at inciting some of the impressionable students. One clear example is when I received an unsolicited or random email from a white female student. "Hey Noyoo," read the email. "You should do 1, 2, 3." Copied in on the email was the "counsellor". I was really taken aback. First, I did not need tutorials on how to run a department from a student whom I was teaching and who was grappling with policy analysis in one of the courses I was teaching. An undergraduate student should have focussed on her assignments and not on schooling me on how to run an academic department. Second, I was not her friend or peer, for her to address me by surname without a prefix. Moreover, if people are on a friendly basis, they address each other by their first names.

I told her not to rudely engage with me, but she was adamant and wanted a dialogue with me and responded that I had insisted on being called Noyoo in class. I said to her that if she was used to addressing her black African garden boys or kitchen boys at home by their surnames, I was not her helper. She then said I insisted on being called Professor, and thus she would escalate the matter to the Dean. I told her to go ahead! I now knew what was at play and who had sent her.

Two days later, another random email was sent by a black African male student who told me how examination marks should be tabulated. Who was copied in this communication email? You guessed right! None other than the "counsellor"! I did not bother to respond to this student. The insults and demeaning interaction had extended to students. However, the majority of the students had yearned for transformation and progress and supported my agenda. It was clear to see this. This is what got me going, together with the support from the hard-working colleagues.

So, I was against the ropes as the dean and her cohorts had managed to do this through an incessant and corrosive campaign against me. I was charged with all manner of infractions, including refusing to teach a course that was not mine. When I became HoD I never asked the staff to do things I did not do. I wanted to lead from the front. Therefore, when some academics complained of heavy teaching loads, I took on extra courses to show that I was with them. As an HoD I had a heavy teaching load. My predecessor's or other HoD's workloads at the time were minuscule compared to mine.

One day, I received an email from the faculty manager asking if I could help avert a crisis relating to students who had registered late. She asked me if the department could make a concession and allow the students to attend classes. However, at this juncture the Honours block was in its second week. When I asked the staff for their inputs via the internal email, no one was the least interested in proffering a solution, especially the lecturer who taught the course (the one who spoke on top of her voice). I thus volunteered to teach a course that belonged to her (because the Honours students had registered late).

After teaching the first block, I thought that the said lecturer would continue teaching her course. It was a temporary arrangement, as I was in fact helping the university avert a crisis. After the faculty manager had reached out to the department and me, the HoD, I had volunteered to take on this extra class. However, when this lecturer insisted that I should continue

   Surviving a University Department from Hell

teaching these students separately, I refused. This issue was rushed to the dean by the cited lecturer. Again, I had to explain why I had "refused to teach a course". I was besides myself when I got this communication from the dean. Really? This was not my course in the first place! I had volunteered so as to help the university ward off a crisis and here I was being punished for doing this! This was on top of my high teaching load and my HoD, as well as other academic responsibilities.

This was not the first time I had taken on a class that was not mine. After a lecturer refused to teach a course, I would volunteer and pick up that course. There was one lecturer who was part of the Gang of Six who had a propensity to just drop courses when she felt that she could not cope in delivering them. And she would be indulged while using this as a grievance.

Due to the highly toxic environment, my health had begun deteriorating at this stage. In fact, as I am writing this book I am getting annoyed at UCT for abusing me the way it did. This was not fair! Anyhow, this issue formed part of the disciplinary charges of "dereliction" against me, which were lodged by the dean. I remembered one thing: as my health took a turn for the worse, my doctor had put me on bed rest. The dean had dragged me out of my sick bed with her famous callouts to meet me on the 4th of January 2020 for her famous "step down sermons". There was no sense of compassion or empathy exercised by this individual. This abuse formed part of my grievances against her. However, the system was rigged and the DVC (teaching and learning), who was also her friend, did not find her culpable. After my grievance, I knew that the dean would come after me with everything that she had.

To begin with, the dean levelled charges against me and then asked the VC at the time to suspend me from the position of HoD. The VC's communication pertaining to my suspension read in part:

Dear Associate Professor Noyoo

PROPOSED SUSPENSION FROM DUTIES AS HEAD OF DEPARTMENT

I write to advise that the University has become aware of certain allegations against you relating to inter alia, the dereliction of your duties in the Department of... and being party to the publication of an article in the City Press (dated 22 March 2020) potentially bringing the department in disrepute.

This letter serves to inform you that the matter has been referred to a Preliminary Investigation Committee (PIC) in respect of the allegations currently pending against you. As a result, I am considering suspending you from your position as Head of the Department until after the PIC dismisses the allegations, refers the case for consideration to a Committee of Inquiry or determines the matter upon agreed terms. Unless you are able to justify why you should not be suspended from the Head of Department position until after the PIC process has been concluded, the suspension will be with immediate effect.

At that juncture in my working life, I had never been suspended for anything. I said to myself, "To hell with this HoD nonsense!" I then resigned from the HoD position with immediate effect. However, despite resigning, the spurious charges that had been levelled against me still stood.

The charges against me were the following:

- *Dereliction of your duties and responsibilities as the Head of Department (HoD) ("first allegation")*
- *Dereliction of your duties and responsibilities and uncollegial behaviour as a member of a department ("second allegation") and*
- *Being party to the publishing of a media article in the City Press,[26] potentially placing the Faculty and University into disrepute by bringing into public domain ongoing internal processes ("third allegation").*

The so-called uncollegial behaviour charge did not even consider the views or inputs of the serious academics and senior administrator. My "colleagues" were only the Gang of Six. These individuals had exhibited highly unprofessional, crass and uncouth behaviour. I responded to the VC in the following manner:

Department of ....
Cape Town
Upper Campus Tel:
Leslie Social Sciences Building Fax:
Rondebosch
7701
South Africa
9 June 2020

The Vice Chancellor
Professor...

---

26 Mdakane, B. & Fengu, M. (2022). *UCT Academics at war*. Retrieved https://www.news24.com/citypress/news/uct-academics-at-war-20200324

Dear Professor....,

Re: Response to Allegations of Serious Misconduct and Proposed Suspension as Head of Department (HOD)

I am writing this letter in response to allegations of serious misconduct and dereliction of duties related to my role as HoD, as well as being party to the publication of an article in the City Press dated 22 March 2020. First, I would like to deny all these allegations. Second, I did not author and I was not party to an article that was written by a City Press journalist.

Nevertheless, I am putting it on record that this is the first time I have been made aware of my supposed misconduct. The dean, as my line manager, never communicated to me, either verbally or in writing, any concerns she had regarding my supposed careless neglect of my duties. I, on the other hand, had engaged her on my health situation, whereby I raised my concerns that I could not continue taking on extra teaching loads for other staff members who chose not to teach certain courses. The attached document refers to the said communication.

Furthermore, it is also important to contextualise the first allegation. I have not been a sole HoD for close to two years. In this regard, I have overseen operational matters and procedures of the department with the deputy HoD who has played specific roles on a daily basis. Remunerations attached to this post are also shared accordingly. I specifically created the deputy HoD position to make sure that there was a smooth running of the department, should something happen to the HoD. To this end, the deputy HOD has been an acting HoD since 13 May 2020. To my knowledge, the dean has never expressed any disquiet regarding this situation to me, either verbally or in writing.

   Surviving a University Department from Hell

Furthermore, the above mentioned situation resonates with the social contract that I made with the staff of the Department of ..., regarding my tenure, in 2018. Records will show that I made an undertaking to colleagues that six months before my term as HoD ended, I would have stepped aside to play a diminished role in the department. The rationale for this stance was to allow for a smooth transition. Therefore, the proposed decision to suspend my duties as HoD should take this reality into critical consideration.

However, it must be put on record that the manner in which these allegations have been levelled against me leaves much to be desired. This is because in more serious circumstance, the dean, and even the deputy vice chancellor – teaching and learning, outrightly refused to investigate certain errant staff members of the Department of ...., when I had wanted to institute disciplinary measures against them. One of them is a known staff member of the department who allegedly smoked drugs in his office and was at the centre of the burning of an office in the Robert Leslie Social Science Building. He did this, notwithstanding the university's non-smoking policy. Despite overwhelming evidence from camera footage, campus security eyewitness accounts and a history of smoking in the department, which predates my appointment, the dean and the deputy vice chancellor – teaching and learning flatly refused to engage with this matter.

Also, the dean and the deputy vice chancellor – teaching and learning did not want to discipline another staff member who verbally abused and threatened me in a staff meeting. Despite staff meeting recordings and eyewitness accounts, this lecturer was never disciplined. She even went on to abuse a prospective disabled student. This matter was investigated and referred to the Faculty of Humanities and my office, by the office of the deputy vice chancellor – transformation. Still, she has not been disciplined. Both individuals were never referred to a Preliminary Investigating Committee (PIC).

It is noteworthy that the university should apply its disciplinary rules uniformly and fairly because the two cited cases, which are entwined with my case, were never even considered by the dean and deputy vice chancellor – teaching and learning. That is why I had lodged formal grievances against the dean. Curiously, she is the one who has now levelled charges of gross misconduct against me. It is important that due process is followed when disciplinary charges are levelled against any academic at the University of Cape Town (UCT). Given the foregoing, I can surmise that the PIC process has not only been weaponised by some executive officers of the Faculty of …, but it is something that seems to target individuals who fit a certain predetermined and preconceived criterion in the Department of ….

Sincerely,
Ndangwa Noyoo

I appeared in front of the Preliminary Investigating Committee (PIC) virtually, as this was during the COVID-19 pandemic. This committee had indeed found most of the charges spurious and dismissed them and only stuck to the newspaper article. After they made their findings, the then VC, despite knowing the issues I had raised to her in my letter, which were cited by the newspaper article, asserted:

"The PIC has concluded on the 07th of September 2020 that after due consideration not to pursue charges against you in relation to the first and second allegations against you, however, that there is prima facie evidence of misconduct in relation to the third allegation. In this regard the PIC recommends that a

    Surviving a University Department from Hell

Committee of Inquiry (COI) be established to test the allegation against you." (sic)

I must underline the fact that in all my working life I had not faced any disciplinary action. I always kept my nose clean and worked hard, as I believed that hard work paid off (I still believe that it does). This was the first time I found myself in such a position, and it was an unsettling experience. I could also discern that the agenda here was to dismiss me, and indeed at this stage I had lost faith in all UCT processes.

I then engaged my lawyers to represent me at the COI. Indeed, as I had suspected with my lawyers, the university was gunning for dismissal. Not because I had maliciously damaged university property, not because I was smoking drugs in my office, not because I had engaged in arson. No! But because I was deemed "uncollegial", among other silly charges! The person who had done such things and was even caught on CCTV camera but, even with so much overwhelming prima facie evidence against him, has never been brought in front of a PIC and COI! To date, nothing has happened to him. In fact, he was promoted to HoD. Before I left the university he was being protected by the dean, new DVC, HR, and the new interim vice chancellor. I will elaborate on this issue in the next chapter.

After a gruelling process, my lawyer managed to take the dismissal item off the table. Members of the COI then said that I should apologise to the university through a written letter and that I should not engage in actions that had brought me to the COI for one year. My lawyer refused, as this was tantamount to an admission of guilt. However, I was so exhausted and wanted to just get on with my life. So, I told my lawyer that I would write the letter.

After resigning from the position of HoD and after writing the letter, I thought that I would quietly focus on my work and that the Gang of Six and their supporters would leave me alone. Oh boy, was I wrong! They were just getting started!

Despite having written this letter of apology, I want to publicly retract my apology and emphatically state in this book that *UCT is a xenophobic (mainly targeting sub-Saharan black African academics and other professionals) and racist institution!* UCT should not have pinned me into a corner and forced me to apologise for stating the obvious, that it is a racist institution. It had even admitted to this reality in its own final report which was completed by its own Institutional Reconciliation and Transformation Commission (IRTC). Among other issues, the report states the following:

On the basis of submissions received and an analysis of policies and other documents, we have, reluctantly, concluded that racism does exist at UCT, that it goes beyond attitudes and beliefs and is aided and abetted by poor management systems which administratively result in discrimination on a racial basis. It is worth noting that not a single submission claimed that UCT is not a racist place. Racism at the University of Cape Town often demonstrates itself in subtle forms of daily micro-aggressions, which however have an impact equal to a direct and explicit racial discrimination.[27]

Is it any wonder that my tenure of HoD was deliberately sabotaged by a white man who was at the centre of burning an office and maliciously damaging public property while smoking drugs at the workplace, and yet he was and continues

---

27 For the full report, follow this link: https://www.news.uct.ac.za/downloads/ irtc/IRTC_Final_Report_2019.pdf

   Surviving a University Department from Hell

to be supported by the entire institution while I was not? Is this not racism? In terms of my outputs and what I had secured UCT as an HoD and my CV, the aforementioned individual's contributions and academic qualifications pale in comparison to mine. But here I was, hounded at every turn by non-performers, just because they celebrated this white man with questionable behaviour, no ethics, and dubious academic achievements.

At this stage I had applied for full professorship via an ad hominem process. As a courtesy, one could approach the dean for him or her to make an assessment whether an academic should go ahead with the process or not. In my case, the dean appointed an "independent assessor", who recommended to the dean that "I was not ready" and should wait for two more years before I could submit my application. This "assessment" was predictable and nauseating, to say the least. I asked myself when these people were going to stop putting obstacles in my way.

One thing these individuals did not know was that I had already started putting together my portfolio of evidence and sharpening my teaching philosophy before I even came to UCT, as I was already preparing to submit my application for full professor at UJ. I was very conversant with this process and knew which boxes needed to be ticked, so to speak. While the Gang of Six and their supporters were focussing only on destroying my HoD track record, I was busy working and producing good outputs in several areas, including teaching and learning.

I found out at UCT the reason why some black African academics do not get promoted. This is because they actually do not know how the promotion process works or unfolds. Most of the time, it is couched in an esoteric language or shrouded in some "mysterious" discourse. And when it comes to those promotion information sessions, they end up becoming condescending sessions where "accomplished" white academics talk down to black African academics. As I pointed out, I was merely being courteous to the dean (despite all the wrong things she had done to me). Hence, I chose to disregard this erroneous "independent assessment" and submitted my application for full professorship.

I had been around the block before joining UCT and I knew the academic space very well. Some of the people who were busy pursuing me were either in primary or high school when I joined academia after I'd completed my master's degree at Cambridge University. And despite their efforts to block me, I was promoted to full professor. This same situation unfolded when I applied for the National Research Foundation (NRF) scientific rating. This time, it was one of the dean's "enforcers" who had suggested that I should wait another year before I submitted my application. Again, I got rated, even though I had been told not to submit my application.

There is something that I found extremely annoying at UCT. This pertains to insulting black African academics' intelligence. There is a propensity to treat black African academics as imbeciles who are clueless and need to be chaperoned all the time. Assertions such as, "Things are done differently here at UCT," or, "One must know how UCT systems work," are meant to underscore the fact that people of a certain mind-set or orientation are supposed to head portfolios. It was extremely disconcerting and outright annoying to have the Gang of Six telling me what needed to be done for the department when they had nothing to show for themselves as academics. Some had no track records whatsoever in terms of academic outputs, and yet they wanted to instruct me on how to run an academic

   Surviving a University Department from Hell

department. Some wanted me to move from their myopic and clueless template. When I said no, they ganged up against me and launched a vile and vicious campaign against me. However, I knew what needed to be done.

On another note, when I became an HoD I instituted an open-door policy. Literally, I kept my door open. I usually arrived at work around 6:30 or 7AM and did all my HoD administrative work, then focussed on my publications and then prepared for my classes. I would leave the department at either 6:30PM or 7PM. This became my daily routine for almost two and a half years. People would begin arriving at the department at around 8:30AM, 9AM or 9:30AM. By this time, I would be ready for the day. When some of the Gang of Six started arriving around 9AM, they would just saunter into my office, uninvited and without even knocking, which would have been polite, even if the door was open. They would launch into all manner of drivel or irrelevant discussions. They could see that I was busy and could not take a hint when I looked at my computer.

One of them (the one who spoke on top of her voice) nonchalantly waltzed into my office one day and engaged me in her usual irrelevant conversation. I remember that I had a journal article deadline to meet and so I was not in the mood to hear her jabbering away. I vaguely heard what she was saying and just nodded. But she continued and then made a startling and unsettling remark. She noted that the Gang of Six "had my back" and that I should not end up like another black African academic who had committed suicide. This was a big issue at UCT at the time. I looked at her and asked her to leave my office immediately. I told her that she had no right to come into my office to invoke the spirit of suicide to me. I later highlighted this incident in my response to the grievance that was lodged by the Gang of Six. Records are there for all to see.

Another bizarre issue relates to the "counsellor's" insistence on giving me biscuits, coffee, *koeksisters,*[28] or soup in the morning. I always politely refused when she made such offers. The more I refused her food and drinks, the more she insisted on offering them to me. Until one day in frustration she exclaimed, "You really do not want to accept my coffee or biscuits!" I said that I was fine and had my own coffee for that matter. She was also the one who would walk past my door, greet me and double back and ask, "Are you sure you are alright?" When I said I was fine, she would again pose the same question. This repertoire went on for several months and only ended after the Gang of Six had lodged grievances against me. After many encounters of this nature, and other nasty ones, I started closing my door.

Despite stepping down and working together with other serious colleagues in another department at UTC, where I established a research unit, the Gang of Six and their supporters at faculty level kept on pursuing me and would just not leave me alone. Room to be innovative with peace of mind – later on, to just breathe – was shrinking by the day. I could not breathe at UCT! Life after being an HoD continued to be a nightmare, with a respite only in 2022, when I went overseas for my sabbatical. It was such a pleasure to be appreciated, treated with dignity and respect by colleagues thousands of kilometres away from UCT! I had not felt so free and energised in such a long time!

---

28 This is a sweet sticky South African pastry or some form of doughnut which was brought to the country by the Dutch in 1652.

   Surviving a University Department from Hell

Chapter Four

LIFE AFTER BEING HOD

When I stepped down as HoD there was much glee and delirium from the Gang of Six and their supporters. The delight was palpable, even if we were now engaging via zoom, as COVID-19 was raging across the country and around the world. When one of the Gang of Six was greeted by another, she responded that she was "superbalicious"! (needless to say, such a word does not exist in the English vocabulary, but it goes to show how ecstatic these people were). Indeed, others were already declaring that it was their time, especially when the drug addict and arsonist became the new HoD. However, I am getting ahead of myself here.

In the midst of my so-called disciplinary charges, mentioned earlier, the dean convened a zoom meeting with the staff of the department in question and informed them that I had stepped down (as if the Gang of Six did not know!) and pointed out that there was a need to select an interim HoD. Already, I could discern that this meeting had been choreographed and it was clear where it was going. Also, strategically, the drug addict and arsonist had been asked to sit this one out, as the interim HoD was meant to facilitate his elevation, a year later.

After we found out from the deputy HoD that he was not interested in the HoD position, it was plain sailing for the dean and the Gang of Six. Several names were suggested by the Gang of Six, including one retired HoD (old white man) and one "enforcer". They settled for a white lady who was from the same department as the dean. It was clear to see that they now wanted a white HoD who would roll back the transformation agenda we had tried to implement in the preceding two and a half years.

When the interim HoD took over, she wasted no time in reinstating the "counselling services" that had been terminated during my tenure. This move was met with euphoric acclaims from the Gang of Six. "Counselling services" were back in full swing, and the "counsellor" set out to continue with her work.

Next on the agenda was the watering down of the Institutional Review process and report. The interim HoD then oversaw a sham process of making sure that the report's recommendations were no longer on the department's radar. In line with this thinking, research was removed from the staff meeting agenda. Obviously, this was an appeasement to the Gang of Six who were averse to research and publishing. Then she made sure that the contracts of the older white gentleman and the black African from another African country (who was not a South African like me), were not renewed. These senior scholars formed part of the group that supported me and were serious about their work.

Then she came after me. Suddenly, there a clamour for evaluation of staff performance, even though the Gang of Six had refused to be evaluated for years, and this was something that the dean had completely removed off the table. I knew that something sinister was being hatched. True to form, the interim HoD targeted me and not the non-performing Gang of Six. After her "evaluation", she concluded that I should continue being on probation and not be confirmed as a permanent staff member. It was clear what the agenda was here. As they had been trying to dismiss me, it would be easier to terminate my employment if I were on probation. This "assessment" was well

   Surviving a University Department from Hell

received by one "enforcer", a deputy dean (the same individual who had previously ambushed the staff and hastily convened a meeting to remove me from the HoD position). This was a good assessment, noted the "enforcer" as I had supposedly faced "serious allegations and was uncollegial".

I immediately engaged my lawyers after this travesty. My lawyers and I were able to demonstrate that I had outperformed pretty much everyone in the department for three years and had supporting evidence to prove this. I do not know if the interim HoD had even bothered to look at my performance appraisals (in her hatred and haste), which had been submitted to the dean (as my line manager) and which clearly showed my academic outputs in terms of curriculum development, teaching and learning, student evaluations, publications, social responsiveness, and academic leadership. The former were impeccable and there were no previous challenges that had been highlighted by the dean or the previous acting dean. After the intervention by my lawyers, the DVC (teaching and learning) and HR had no choice but to appoint me a permanent employee of UCT.

After this underhand and diabolical effort had been thwarted, the interim HoD continued on this path of trying to strip me bare of my responsibilities, which were based on my seniority and academic credentials. She also sought to humiliate me and those who had supported me in the department at every given opportunity. In this regard, she appointed a junior academic (the one who spoke on top of her voice) and another newly appointed lecturer (this individual had been fraudulently appointed. I will return to this matter shortly) as postgraduate co-ordinators. The junior academic, who was still struggling to complete her doctoral studies (and still is, even now) and did not have even one publication to her name (not even a newspaper article!) would take pleasure in issuing instructions to me and my colleague from another African country. Emails would be sent to me and my colleague stating, for example: "Ndangwa and X, can you do 1,2,3." I would just shake my head in disbelief. All the Gang of Six were also apportioned senior or co-ordinating roles by this interim HoD. To add insult to injury, my colleague from another African country and I were stripped of most of our policy and development courses and then these were allotted to some members of the Gang of Six.

In one of the many choreographed zoom staff meetings, the interim HoD asked one member from the Gang of Six (the one who dropped courses whenever she felt, for whatever reason, that she did not want to teach them) to present something related to the teaching of postgraduate courses. In her introduction, she noted that "the dean said anyone can teach any course". These are individuals who never researched, published in the area, or arguably knew the content.

I tried to challenge this unjust move and resist this new wave of humiliation. My colleague from another African country sent me a text and advised me to "let it go". Indeed, the situation was futile and I kept quiet after this.

Then, some of their badly conceptualised courses were given to me. However, as this book was going to press, the same individual stated in a staff meeting that she was struggling to teach the same courses she had forced herself to teach, with the help of the former interim HoD and the dean. That is, in the way that the courses had been initially constituted. She suggested that the courses be changed. The arsonist and drug addict concurred, and this matter was tabled at a postgraduate committee meeting.

Guess what? The changes to the course, which mirrored the deficits of the aforementioned lecturer, were swiftly accepted by the postgraduate committee. This committee is populated by their friends and anything that is tabled there by the Gang of Six is accepted. Therefore, courses could be changed willy-nilly to suit the inabilities and incompetencies of particular lecturers, while they were being watered down in the process. There is nothing wrong with recurriculating, but not at the expense of quality. I had reported this matter to the interim VC in my grievance against the drug addict and arsonist. This grievance was essentially put on ice by the said individual.

In pursuit of this nefarious scheme, a job for a doctoral student, who was also a recruit of the Gang of Six, was created. This is part of the corrupt practices at UCT, which I had reported to the interim VC in my grievance against the drug addict and arsonist and which were never attended to. After elbowing out two academics from the group of the hard-working and serious colleagues, the interim HoD, the Gang of Six, their supporters such as the dean, and others created a post for their young proxy. These were some of the young people who wanted to be academics but wanted to use short-cuts and hence became the "foot soldiers" of the Gang of Six in their "war" against people like me. They were black African South Africans.

I discovered that this was a general practice in other parts of UCT, whereby black Africans either from South Africa or other African countries would be recruited and be used as tokens to show-case its "transformation" efforts. In the latter case, the black Africans from other African countries are mainly those with the "I have arrived" mentality. Thus, these two categories of black Africans would be the ones doing the bidding of the white and racist management. Malcom X referred to such blacks as *house negroes*[29] and in South African liberation parlance, such individuals were known as *impipis* or *askaris*. There are many of these black Africans running around UCT and beguiling the country that there is transformation taking place at this university and yet patriarchy, white privilege and white hegemony are being protected and nurtured.

These black Africans are even more dangerous than racist white people because, just like the house Negro or *impimpi*, they derail progress in fundamental ways while purporting to

---

29 According to Malcom X: To understand this, you have to go back to what is referred to as the house Negro and the field Negro during slavery. There were two kinds of slaves, the house Negro and the field Negro. The house Negroes – they lived in the house with master, they dressed pretty good, they ate good because they ate his food – what he left. They lived in the attic or the basement, but still they lived near their master; and they loved their master more than their master loved himself. They would give their life to save their master's house – quicker than the master would. If the master said, "We got a good house here," the house Negro would say, "Yeah, we got a good house here." Whenever the master said "we," he said "we." That is how you can tell a house Negro. If the master's house caught on fire, the house Negro would fight harder to put the blaze out than the master would. If the master got sick, the house Negro would say, "What's the matter, boss, we sick?" We sick! He identified himself with his master, more than his master identified with himself. And if you came to the house Negro and said, "Let's run away, let's escape, let's separate." The house Negro would look at you and say, "Man, you crazy. What you mean, separate? Where is there a better house than this? Where can I wear better clothes than this? Where can I eat better food than this?" That was the house Negro. In those days he was called a "house nigger". And that's what we call them today, because we've still got some house niggers running around here. Source: X, Malcolm. "Message to the Grass Roots." Northern Negro Grass Roots Leadership Conference. Group on Advanced Leadership. King Solomon Baptist Church, Detroit. 10 November 1963. Cited from: Columbia Centre for Teaching and Learning, on this link: https://ccnmtl.columbia.edu/projects/mmt/mxp/speeches/mxa29.html

    Surviving a University Department from Hell

be fighting together with their black and African brothers and sisters, but selling them out to UCT management in the process. Some of them are just "baas[30] boys" or "baas girls" and would do anything that their white masters tell them to do. Even if it is against progress or transformation. Such blacks at UCT would use structures such as the Black Academic Caucus (BAC) as stepping stones to get into bigger and loftier positions in the university. Others sit on or head "transformation" committees and simply rubber stamp decisions made by management. I had joined this BAC and, after a short spell, resigned, as it was populated by reactionary individuals who formed the core group that supported the Gang of Six and persecuted me at UCT. How could they preach transformation when they were harassing an accomplished black African scholar like me? Frankly, I was nauseated by their hypocrisy.

This job for the young crony of the Gang of Six was hastily "manufactured" by the Interim HoD and her Gang of Six. We, who were treated as imbeciles, could see what was going on and knew exactly what their plan was, even if they thought that we were stupid. As things turned out, we were right, as the whole selection process was rigged: from individuals who sat on the selection panel to the way others who were not part of this clique were barred from participating in the said process. It was very clear to ascertain what the end goal was for this so-called selection process.

There were five candidates who had applied for this position. Two had no doctoral degrees (one of them was the preferred individual who eventually got the job, and the other individual was the only male on the list) while the rest had

---

30 This means boss in Afrikaans.

doctoral degrees (PhDs), with one of them even lecturing in a prestigious university overseas. The candidates were asked to deliver a fifteen-minute presentation explaining from their disciplinary position how they saw the role of their discipline "in the challenges we face in South Africa today. Explain how your research would contribute to this." This question was not only ambiguous and unclear, but it lacked rigour as well as depth. Anyhow, let me return to the issue at hand. The whole process was shrouded in secrecy, as it was only the Gang of Six and their supporters who were privy to it. After the sham window dressing exercise, we were all informed that the young crony of the Gang of Six had got the job and was the best candidate. As usual, the congratulatory messages via the internal mailing system were resounding and deafening.

I did not engage in such hypocritical antics but reached out to a former colleague who had been hounded from the department by the Gang of Six (also a black African from another African country) and was working at another university. He was also the former supervisor and mentor of one of the candidates who had been shortlisted. This young, female and black African South African was a product of the department in question and we knew how intelligent and hard-working she was. She had won various fellowships and had even interned at a prestigious organisation in the United States. She was also an expert in quantitative research (an area that this department seriously lacked) and she was already published. This young, female, black, African, South African scholar was teaching in the United Kingdom and had wanted to come back to her home country and contribute to its development. Just because she was not associated with the Gang of Six, she was denied this opportunity to be a lecturer at UCT. I was quite infuriated with this level of

                        Surviving a University Department from Hell

corruption. In my view, and that of other colleagues who were not part of the Gang of Six, she was the best candidate. I was not going to let such a travesty just slide. Enough was enough, I thought!

After speaking to my former colleague, I then contacted the young scholar and asked for her sentiments on why UCT had not picked her. This is what she had to say:

Dear Professor Noyoo,

Good to hear from you. I am well, thanks.

Aaah! I was a bit disappointed, but I am over it now. I didn't get the job. I don't have a problem with losing to a fellow scholar on par in terms of qualifications and experience. Their decision indirectly communicated that a UCT PhD is worth less than a UCT Master's degree. I didn't get a satisfactory answer when I inquired about which criteria I did not meet for the job. I was later invited to apply for a three-year fixed-term contract position when I was denied a permanent position. So, I declined the invitation to apply for the fixed-term contract because it didn't make sense to me. I doubt that when I decide to come back to SA, UCT will be my first choice. I kept up with the staff page to see who got the job and, no disrespect to the colleague, but in terms of qualifications, HE teaching experience, international exposure, community engagement and publications, my CV will show that I am more experienced. If I am being honest, it appeared/felt to me that the decision to employ the person was made before the interviews were conducted.

At the time of my application, I was a Master of... lecturer at the University of ... in the United Kingdom. Towards the end of last year, I got a job at the University of ... as a senior lecturer in .... I am really enjoying it at my new job. I have had quite a couple of publications over the past two years, and I am working on more. I am really focusing on building my publication profile and it's going well. Just this month, I submitted two book chapter contributions in collaboration with colleagues in the UK and the USA, and I am working on an article with colleagues in the USA to submit by the end of this month. I also have other papers lined up with Prof ... to submit before the end of the year. I am very grateful for Professor ...'s continued mentorship. He doesn't have to, he could have easily cut ties with me after I finished my PhD, but he continues to be a great mentor and an invaluable sounding board as I progress in my career. I am in a good place and have no hard feelings towards my alma mater!

My CV is attached.
Best wishes,

One of the issues I had highlighted to UCT management when I had rebutted the grievances of the Gang of Six in 2018 was how unqualified these individuals were to even be university lecturers. Where did the university get these individuals? How were they recruited? I also wanted to find out how they had been promoted to positions of senior lecturer and associate professor with such paltry and shoddy outputs. Here were lecturers who were studying for PhDs together with their students for many years and had not completed their PhDs, while their students had done so. How could they properly instruct students? These lecturers could not unpack and teach the core content in the department's curriculum and yet they expected students to exhibit depth in the former. How could this be? As things still

    Surviving a University Department from Hell

stand, they just go and read slides to students or make them watch videos.

However, I discovered later that jobs in the department were crafted for friends or particular persons they had chosen. Indeed, jobs for pals is an entrenched practice at UCT that has HR, academic departments, and the faculty I am focussing on in this book at the centre of such maleficence. I cannot speak for other faculties. This is evidence that I presented in my grievances against the drug addict and arsonist to the interim vice chancellor and he never bothered to test it. With hindsight, I am not surprised that he was not enthused about fighting corruption at UCT as he seemed tainted himself and was already linked to a possible scandal by the press.[31]

Anyhow, this corrupt practice of jobs for pals is intertwined with the promotion of undeserving students to master's or doctoral programmes.

Another student who did the Gang of Six's bidding and who had performed miserably at Honours level was somehow now a Master's candidate. The interim HoD was working on overdrive to enforce all the wishes of the Gang of Six. And who was this student's supervisor? Surprise, surprise, it was none other than the co-anchor of the Gang of Six. The female academic who

---

31 Hlat, S. (2023) reports: UCT has refuted allegations of nepotism after it came to light that interim Vice-Chancellor Professor Daya Reddy was the brother-in-law of Registrar Royston Pillay. Reddy was appointed in March following former Vice-Chancellor Mamokgethi Phakeng's departure from the university. However, the institution says this was declared upfront and had no influence on his appointment, which was based on his academic standing and the strong leadership qualities. See more by clicking on this link: https://www.iol.co.za/capetimes/news/nepotism-claims-uct-council-wants-investigation-into-leaks-75904759-ea27-43bb-ac9e-543cdb1e57f0

had insulted, threatened and demeaned me in a staff meeting! This is how this group and their supporters operated: almost like a cult or criminal cartel. When one of them was exposed, they all closed ranks around him or her. They also rewarded each member who had helped them to execute their misdeeds. Therefore, what would make young and aspiring academics want to spend long hours in libraries, like us, researching and looking for information, when they could easily join a cult or criminal cartel at UCT and be quickly rewarded?

Another incident that exposed the unethical and corrupt behaviour of the drug addict and arsonist was when the departmental Ethics Committee had vetted his research proposal and sent him pointed issues that he had to address so that the committee could give him the go-ahead to collect data. His proposal was shallow, porous and did not make the cut. I sat on that committee. We asked him to strengthen his proposal and made specific recommendations. The matter was referred to the new Chair of the Ethics Committee (at this juncture, all the senior academics who were not part of the Gang of Six had been stripped of the co-ordinating roles in the department by the interim HoD). After some time, when we did not get any response from the Chair regarding the said proposal, the senior academic who was about to retire reminded me to follow up on the issue. Strangely, on the same day on ResearchGate (a network that connects academics, researchers and students all over the world), the drug addict and arsonist had posted a new "research study" on which he had embarked. This is the same research study that did not get ethical clearance! I informed my colleagues about this new development. We were flabbergasted! This individual was indeed a fraud and a conman. We wanted

                           Surviving a University Department from Hell

answers and this is how the communications unfolded when we wanted to get to the truth:

Hello Y (the Chair),

A few meetings ago we considered an ethics approval request from…. We decided that it needed to be revised and resubmitted. Have we had it back yet? This came to mind when reading …. fourth research project.

Thanks,

X (the white serious and senior colleague)

I responded to the above email in this way:

Thanks, X, for picking this up.

I had totally forgotten about it. Y (the Chair), the committee did not get anything back from…, despite all of us spending precious hours on the said document. An update is of crucial importance.

Thanks,

Ndangwa

When the Committee's Chair did not respond to our emails, I followed up in this way:

Dear Y,

Sorry, but you have not provided us an answer regarding…. (the individual's) resubmit.

Kind regards,

Ndangwa

Finally, after being evasive, the Chair responded to our queries in this manner:

Dear Colleagues

I formally contacted… regarding the amendments with the recommendation to amend and re-submit of the panel.

… was resistant to the amendments and to re-submit.

After a formal discussion, with him I was informed of external factors

1. *The project was externally funded and there were deadlines for ethical approval*
2. *The potential loss of external funding*
3. *The project had been considerably delayed already*

After my discussion with… and the above external factors I was compelled and persuaded to sign off the ethics application.

Kind regards
Y

I responded to the Chair's email in a formal manner, as I could see that this matter was serious and was going to be swept under the rug. I knew that these issues would be of consequence in the future when people would be asked to account:

Dear Dr. Y,

May my communication with you be minuted for future correspondence and engagement? Having been the one who introduced a Higher Degrees Committee (HDC) type of "Ethics Committee" when I was HoD, I would like to place it on record that this decision does not sit well with me. I feel disrespected and disregarded. Also, it now makes sense why the HDC has been diluted to this fragmented structure – so that some staff in this department can engage in unethical behaviour as attested by …. [the drug addict and arsonist's] actions. Mind you, his documents were already signed when we interrogated them.

… cannot use the committee as a "rubber stamping" body. We applied ourselves diligently and impartially to the task that was at hand. Those comments were not for him but for his student. Furthermore, if he had any challenges with our inputs, he could have engaged us, in the same manner that all of us do when we have queries pertaining to our students' proposals. I submit to you that when I was HoD I made sure that such structures were above board and transparent, and that academic fraud could not be perpetrated via such structures. This episode is indeed extremely unfortunate and highly disappointing.

Kind regards,
A/Prof Ndangwa Noyoo

It is important to note that, even if a research study is externally funded, it must be given a stamp of approval by an ethics committee. One cannot just go and undertake research that has all sorts of breaches, including ethical ones, just because it is externally funded. Really? The interim HoD had been copied into all the above correspondence. Perhaps she had thought that this matter would just go away. When we continued probing and saw that things were getting hot, she responded in this manner:

Dear colleagues,

I would urge you, when there is a difference of opinion, to discuss the matter with each other, rather than sending emails – they really are not helpful.

I have asked Dr Y to send me all the documents in this case and will review them myself.

Best,
So and so...

This was not a difference of opinion! A so-called senior academic had breached the canons of research by going ahead with a study that was not sanctioned by the department's Ethics Committee. Come on! Who did this lady think she was dealing with? Academic novices? When the interim HoD had seen that the drug addict and arsonist had wantonly broken the rules of academia and scientific research, she went full throttle to cover this serious infraction. She proposed that the department should convene an "ethics workshop". For what purpose, I thought? I still do not know to this day. But here we were,

Surviving a University Department from Hell

serious academics, being talked down to and our intelligence being insulted in the process because she wanted to cover up for the drug addict and arsonist. He should have faced disciplinary action. But since he was part of the "cult" or "criminal cartel" at UCT, he was a "made man" and an untouchable. The interim HoD insulted our intelligence further in this manner, in an email which was sent to all staff members:

Dear colleagues,

If you have any ethics queries that you'd like... to address in the workshop tomorrow, please send them through to me. I've one of my own (about working with high school learners in the era of POPIA), but you may be heading into a project where you'd like some ethics advice. Tomorrow is the ideal time to pick .... brains, so let's use it!

Best,
So and so...

None of us who were serious academics attended this nonsensical workshop. To this day, this unethical incident remains buried. However, I did report this matter to the interim VC in my grievance against the drug addict and arsonist. Nonetheless, before the interim HoD's term expired she first dished out sabbaticals to the Gang of Six. These individuals had previously gone on sabbaticals and come back with no academic outputs... nothing! How they qualified to go on sabbaticals willy-nilly beats me, but I know that there is money that covers such endeavours. Usually, this is derived from subsidies that lecturers bring to the university through their publications, grants and other research outputs. Since these individuals did not publish, where was the money coming from to cover their academic leave? This could only mean that the few of us who were publishing were also working and paying for the sabbaticals of the non-performers!

The interim HoD also made sure that the drug addict and arsonist was promoted to the HoD position. To make this process as smooth as possible, she approached the former deputy HoD to stand down and not show interest in the position. He refused and threw his hat into the ring, so to speak. However, this process was again rigged. One could easily discern where this process was going. The dean informed us that the process would be dependent on the "show of hands". It was obvious that we were outnumbered by the Gang of Six and they would vote for their *baas*. Those of us who had not been part of the shenanigans could not outvote this group.

At that juncture, one hard-working young white academic, who had supported me switched allegiances when she saw the pendulum had decisively swung in the direction and favour of the Gang of Six. Her fawning emails to the interim HoD and the Gang of Six, which were also laced with subtle ridicule aimed at me, were nauseating to say the least. But I did not blame her as she had to cover herself against the onslaught of the Gang of Six. Not everyone can "die" for their principles like some of us.

After this, another "enforcer" of the dean was appointed to oversee the "selection" of the drug addict and arsonist. Once I saw another of the Dean's "enforcers" overseeing this process, I knew for sure that it was rigged, and it was deliberately tilted in favour of the drug addict and arsonist. I boycotted the selection process and did not even bother to respond to the emails from the "enforcer" asking me to cast my vote. After this, the drug addict and arsonist was "unanimously" voted as the next HoD.

Thankfully, my nine-month sabbatical was approved (after several hurdles had been thrown in my way. This, even though I was the most published academic in this department!). I just wanted to leave this toxic environment and focus on my work. Interestingly, UCT did not even give me a cent for my sabbatical. All expenses, including flights, accommodation and upkeep, were covered by my hosts in Europe. This, despite bringing so much money to UCT via my publications. What a joke! I thought to myself. So, I did not care whether the drug addict and arsonist was the new HoD.

The celebrations from the Gang of Six and newly recruited members from the ranks of the administration personnel were "deafening". In their thanks to the outgoing interim HoD the Gang of Six and their new recruits peddled veiled insults aimed at me and the serious and hard-working colleagues. We were informed how the Gang of Six drew "inspiration" from the Interim HoD's "quiet and steady leadership". The dean also thanked the interim HoD for a "stellar job". Obviously, such sentiments were meant to show that the black, African academic from another African country had been loud and abrasive and had failed to perform.

This group is very good at spinning lies and slanderous remarks, and then turning them into a person's narrative. That is why I chose to write this book because I was not going to allow individuals with highly questionable characters and ethics to spin me into a nonsensical narrative. Let the court of South African public opinion as well courts of law decide and not the kangaroo courts at UCT!

Once the drug addict and arsonist had been rewarded, the co-anchor of the Gang of Six (who had insulted and threatened me in a staff meeting) was also rewarded with a plum position at the faculty by the dean. The dean's corruption was clearly evident here because we were informed that this individual was going on another sabbatical! (I think that it was the fourth one she was taking). As this book was going to press, her sabbatical had been extended for another year! Wow! It pays to belong to a cult or criminal cartel at UCT!

How can someone who hardly publishes and has shoddy academic outputs first, go on sabbaticals anyhow? Secondly, how can such as academic be "seconded" to faculty and enjoy the perks of a plum job, when she was supposed to be on sabbatical, researching and developing herself? Remember the double-dipping story I related earlier, which pertained to these individuals who were overseeing a provincial government's project, while paying themselves "salaries" and which I questioned and put on ice? Well, here we are again, double dipping. The stench of corruption and maladministration at this faculty is suffocating.

The year 2021 ended with the Gang of Six and their handlers and supporters in triumphant ascendance. My other two serious colleagues had been elbowed out of the department. There were only two black, African and serious academics left in the department. One was South African, and one was from another African country.

As I was jumping on the plane and flying off to Europe, I looked out of the window and said a little prayer to the Lord for looking after me in all the turbulent years at UCT. If it was not for God Almighty, I would have been toast, as they say. I also made a decision there and then that I would not accept being

Surviving a University Department from Hell

tortured and demeaned by the drug addict and arsonist and his minions, the dean, and the rest of UCT. I was ready to leave that toxic and useless place.

My sabbatical was a blast and awesome, as my children would say. I loved the collegiality (in the true sense of the word!), intellectual depth and rigour and high-level academic engagements I was exposed to in Europe. It was such a pleasure to stay away from that echo chamber of a department that was underwritten by high levels of mediocrity. I also travelled across the European country I was based in and presented academic papers and engaged with various scholars at different universities. I was invited to present papers at various symposia and even lecture at different universities across Europe.

For a while, I thought that I would be left alone. However, after June 2022, I received an email from the drug addict and arsonist in his capacity as HoD to submit a form related to my performance. Here is a man, who had beat the biggest drum against staff performance appraisals for four years and non-stop, asking me to engage in such a process and while I was on sabbatical. I chose to not recognise this individual. I did not respond to him and never did (this formed part of his so-called disciplinary charges, which I will get to in a short while).

As the year was closing, I got another irritating email from the drug addict and arsonist, asking me for my teaching load and to indicate which courses I was going to teach in 2023. I knew exactly what was afoot. He was extending the pernicious agenda of the interim HoD of stripping me of my courses. I wondered why this individual was doing this because there was an unwritten rule in that department, whereby the courses that an individual taught when he or she was on sabbatical should not be tinkered with. I for one had not touched the courses that the drug addict and arsonist taught when he was on "sabbatical", which basically meant him coming to the department daily to disrupt its operations through a concerted campaign against me and burning an office while smoking drugs. I did not answer him (again this formed part of his so-called disciplinary charges against me). As far as I was concerned, this chap was an illegal and illegitimate HoD. I was not going to take drug-induced instructions from him, no matter how much HR, the dean and UCT management tried to sanitise and legitimise him, and force him on me. I was on the war path. I would never say *ja baas*[32] to this chap! Never!

When I came back to South Africa after my sabbatical in Europe, and after I resumed duties when the academic year started in February 2023, I knew that I was going to be defiant and radical all the way. I also made sure that this time, when I engaged with whomever, I copied various actors into the email communication, so that people would not feign amnesia or even bury the issue altogether. Later, some of them, like the interim VC and his cohorts, would block me. I did not care! I was not going to be cowed and belittled by the callous and racist UCT system.

When I came back, the drug addict and arsonist decided to take away my postgraduate courses and allocated them to none other than? Yes, you guessed right! My courses were going to be taught by the PhD student who had been corruptly and

---

32 Yes boss, in Afrikaans. Black Africans were expected to address white people like this during apartheid, even when they were not their actual bosses. Even some white children of the time expected black African adults to address them as baas or madam.

                    Surviving a University Department from Hell

fraudulently employed by UCT. I then lodged grievances against the drug addict and arsonist. Predictably, the dean came back and informed me that the matter would be overseen by her "enforcer", a deputy dean. Remember the woman who said that even if someone from the Gang of Six had reported that there was a pink pig climbing up the stairs while defecating on them, she would be compelled to investigate? Yes, this individual was again called to do the dean's bidding. I do not know how stupid this dean thought I was.

I refused to have my grievance overseen by this bizarre individual. I said that she was biased and conflicted, based on my previous interactions with her. After my refusal, the dean appointed another friend and "enforcer". This deputy dean had chaired the whole corrupt and fraudulent selection process that saw the Gang of Six's young crony being appointed as a lecturer. At this point I knew that I would not get any justice but wanted to use this process to gather enough evidence that I would later show to relevant and higher authorities, in the higher education sector and other sections of the state, how corrupt and rotten UCT was. So, I just said yes to the dean's sinister proposal.

Thereafter, another sham process unfolded. I was fed up with this racist and sadistic institution. Also, while on sabbatical, when I started getting predictably annoying and demeaning emails from the drug addict and arsonist, with HR being copied in on the correspondence, I knew that he was spoiling for a fight, and I was sure going to give him one! This was my last hurrah! I crafted my grievance in this manner:

I am formally lodging grievances against... in his capacity as the head of department (HoD) of ...

1. Since he became the HoD of the aforementioned department, he has engaged with me in a bullying and disrespectful manner with an intention to intimidate, undermine and humiliate me.

2. .... has presided over the department in a manner that is unilateral and which is underwritten by tenets of corruption, favouritism and maladministration. Such malfeasance is exemplified by the following:

(a) He unilaterally removed me from postgraduate teaching and allotted my courses to a novice who does not have a doctorate degree and does not have meaningful work experience. I, on the other hand, I am a full Professor, with close to thirty years work experience. I have worked at the highest level of policy development and decision-making in government, in the non-governmental sector and academia. This is the experience I bring to academia and the academic project. Furthermore, I am a C2 Rated National Research Foundation (NRF) scientist. I have published widely in the academic areas of .... Diabolically, I am now barred from teaching the courses I was employed to teach at UCT when I was recruited by the university in 2017. Incidentally, I am the one who was employed to overhaul the postgraduate courses and strengthen them by aligning them with undergraduate courses in the two streams of ... and ..., through a scaffolding process.

In addition, I indigenised and de-colonised them. When I asked .... specific questions pertaining to: (i) his reasons for unilaterally removing me from teaching on the postgraduate programme; (ii) if he had undertaken a skills audit when he made the decision to allot my courses to the cited individual (who is also a former student whom he publicly favours); (iii) what imperatives had informed his decision, he categorically refused to answer them

Surviving a University Department from Hell

and declared: "There is a clear breakdown in communication here."

(b) Favouring and creating a tailor-made position to another former favourite student whose skills do not seem to effectively respond to competently teaching and researching in the areas of ....

(c) Supporting his friend's sabbatical application. This individual previously went on sabbatical and came back with no discernible outputs. In fact, this is the general trend in the department where individuals effortlessly and frequently go on sabbaticals and return with no outputs.

3. ... seriously lacks academic leadership and has led a rudderless department which is bereft of research and publication outputs. He has not articulated his vision and has not sought to arrive at a vision for the department which is consonant with UCT's Vision 2030. There is no urgency regarding these matters where most staff members have not published for more than five years; do not attend or present at academic conferences or even workshops. When benchmarking the department with other ... departments across South Africa, it can be deciphered that it is the worst performing department. How ironic for a department, which is supposed to be associated with a university that is referred to as "the number one university in Africa".

4. ... has serious failings which disqualify him from being an HoD, later on even an academic. It is not only baffling but mind-numbing that UCT has continued to condone, incentivise and reward his gross misconduct which is characterised by:

- *Smoking drugs at the workplace. This behaviour is known by all his supporters in the department and Faculty of.... For a long time, some staff members complained about his smoking of substances at the workplace, but he has been protected and continues to be protected by UCT (see APPENDIX A).*

- *Due to smoking drugs, he burnt down an office in October 2018. After an investigation by the Campus Protection Services (CPS) was undertaken, it was determined that he was the arsonist who had burnt the office and used drugs in the said office. There is also camera footage that places him at the scene of the crime. This criminal act of arson and malicious damage to university property transpired when he was on sabbatical. If he had used the office for research purposes, as he has claimed, why did CPS find drug paraphernalia in the same office? Why was he using a tiny office that was not allocated to him by the HoD at the time? And why did he not use his big office as he was on sabbatical? Please see the highlighted part in APPENDIX B. To date I have not seen his sabbatical report. I have attached mine for the sake of transparency.*

- *... makes erratic decisions, has a short attention span and is prone to unethical behaviour. In APPENDIX C, the communication pertains to his unethical behaviour, which is linked to his research proposal which was reviewed by the department's Ethics Committee. His research proposal had serious shortfalls and the Committee had advised him to rework it. He did not rework it and went on to publish its findings on the internet as "completed research". This matter was swept under the rug by Professor...,. who was the interim HoD*

   Surviving a University Department from Hell

As I had suspected, the dean's "enforcer" cleared the drug addict and arsonist of any wrongdoing. I was not satisfied and informed the dean that I was going to the second stage of the grievance process. This would now be taken to the VC, in this case the interim VC. At this stage, I had believed that this individual, who was brought back from retirement, to, in my opinion, consolidate and cement patriarchy, white privilege and white hegemony at UCT, would apply himself to this matter, justly and impartially. But this would not be the case. He would actually support the drug addict and arsonist's so-called disciplinary action against me, after I had lodged grievances against him.

No matter how much I pointed out how unprocedural this matter was, given the fact that my grievance was not finalised, the powers that be, including the interim VC, fast-tracked the so-called disciplinary action while my grievance was put on ice. Before I knew it, a so-called disciplinary action was hatched against me, with key proponents being an old white man chairing the process and a young, black African "enforcer" from another African country zealously representing UCT. In my communication to this young man, I asked him what his motive was. Why was he spearheading a sinister agenda that had been hatched at UCT to try to destroy my career? And this was not the first time he had been recruited in a diabolical scheme against me by the dean and her cohorts. I told this young man that none of us came to the Western Cape carrying UCT on our shoulders and that we would all leave UCT one day. We found this institution and we would all leave it.

As for their so-called disciplinary action and call out, this is how I answered them:

Dear All,

I am not coming to your unjust disciplinary hearing that seeks to protect that drug addict and arsonist… at all costs. He destroyed university property as well as endangered the lives of students and staff members in 2018. The burning of an office in Robert Leslie Social Science Building was a public affair, whereby students and staff had to be evacuated.

Furthermore, I caught him intoxicated on drugs the following week with other eyewitnesses. I have reported all these issues to management in the last five years and the records are there for all to see. Now, just because I am a black man, you would rather take his side and not listen to anything I have raised in the last five years. There is overwhelming prima facie evidence and a case against …. Despite this, he has never faced any disciplinary action. But it is fine. I am steadfast in my struggle against injustice and oppression.

It is clear why my grievance against him has not been expedited: because it is on purpose. And here you are, going out of your way to fast track this unjust process. As far as I am concerned, …. is an illegitimate head of department. And you all know that. This is not only shameful, but highly scandalous.

Kind regards,
Professor Ndangwa Noyoo

Thereafter, I informed HR that I was leaving the university with immediate effect. An HR official dealing with such matters responded and informed me that he would inform the dean (acting dean, as the dean had gone on a sabbatical). I thanked him and then informed him that I would wait for the acting dean's response.

After almost two weeks, instead of getting a response related to my immediate departure from UCT, I got an email from the so-called chair of the so-called disciplinary process. His email screamed: **Guilty as Charged!** Really? After two weeks when I had formally informed the university that I was leaving, and with immediate effect? And this is the answer I get? After I had told everyone concerned that I would not attend their useless disciplinary hearing? I was livid. What kind of sadists were these people? I had told them that I was done and I was going. They still went ahead and met and deliberated on the unjust matter? What were these people trying to achieve?

I wrote to HR, informing them, among other things, that after waiting for almost two weeks for a response, so that I could be released and leave UCT, I had got an email informing me of my supposed guilt. I pointed out that my constitutional rights were being violated by these individuals at UCT spearheading these underhand machinations against me. I said that this was highly illegal, and I would be contacting my lawyers. Also, these UCT officials had no right to overrule my decision to leave their toxic university with immediate effect, after I had been subjected to a biased disciplinary process, which I did not attend and where I was charged in absentia.

The HR official informed me that he had been following up on my matter with the acting dean and that he had not got any response yet.

After several days, I was finally informed that I could leave the university but had to wait out another month. After the dust had settled and I had cleared my office and returned the office keys to the department, the dean came back from her sabbatical. Can the reader guess what she did before I left UCT? You guessed right if you were thinking that she was back at her favourite game of summoning me to her office! With barely a few days to go before I left that highly corrosive and poisonous university, I got a "callout" from the dean who had made my life a living hell at UCT. She wanted to meet me and another HR official to discuss the so-called "guilty" charge that had been arrived at while she was on sabbatical. I was beyond incredulity at this point in time and I did not even bother to respond to her email.

This situation with the dean and UCT reminded me of someone who had left a partner in an abusive relationship. I have left you and I do not want to ever see you again, but here you are, sending me messages to meet you. Really? For what? I also pondered accordingly: *Who were these people who jockeyed for such serious and sensitive positions and were awfully cavalier with a lot of people's lives?*[33]

---

33 I like this phrase and actually borrowed it from George Clooney in one of the *Ocean Franchise* movies.

　　　　　Surviving a University Department from Hell

Chapter Five

CONCLUSION

As this book is going to press, I am out of UCT, and I have begun my healing process. I have never been so abused and ill-treated in my life. Even when I was a young activist, being brutalised by an oppressive and tyrannical political system, it was not as bad as this. Also, I think I could deal with the situation much easier (apart from being young and bolstered by an ideal of trying to change the world), because I knew why the system had come after me. Not at UCT! I still want to know why I was shabbily treated when I was doing everything by the book? Why was I so ill-treated when I was merely doing my job?

I had thought hard work paid off. But not at UCT. No matter how much I slaved away for that obnoxious and racist university, I never got anything good in return. I was under siege for five and a half years because some people did not want to do their jobs. I worked day and night, weekends and holidays for that hideous university and got only insults, spit, ridicule, humiliation and disrespect in return, while those who were burning and destroying university property while smoking drugs in offices were rewarded and supported tirelessly by the university management. It was a thankless job! No matter how many international partnerships, or money in the form of student scholarships and publications with their attendant subsidies (money basically), I managed to secure, all I got in return was abuse and disdain. I walked away from something I loved doing because of the ill-treatment I got at UCT.

As things stand, I have decided *to do things my way*, a la Frank Sinatra! I want to categorically apologise to my children for allowing this hideous university and job to take away our family and quality time, for five and a half years!

It is important to note that all the skulduggery that I have reported in this book transpired, and it is being nurtured and entrenched at UCT. However, I must hasten to point out that there are so many wrong things happening across the country's universities. For instance, in 2018, the dean of the Faculty of Arts at the University of Zululand, Professor Gregory Kamwendo, was gunned down in the driveway of his home after uncovering a fraudulent PhD syndicate at his university. One of the accused, who was involved in masterminding his killing, was a lecturer at the same university. He was subsequently sentenced to life imprisonment with his co-accused in 2020.[34] This academic paid with his life for doing his job and doing the right thing!

Recent media reports about the University of Fort Hare paint quite a scary picture. In January 2023, the vice chancellor of the University of Fort Hare, Professor Sakhela Buhlungu, survived an assassination attempt.[35] However, his bodyguard was shot dead. This VC was targeted because he has been at the forefront of a campaign to root out corruption and maleficence at Fort Hare.

---

34 News24 (2020). *Life sentence for murderers of University of Zululand professor*. Retrieved from https://www.news24.com/news24/southafrica/news/life-sentence-for-murderers-of-university-of-zululand-professor-20201017

35 Sangotsha, V. (2023). *Fort Hare vice-chancellor's bodyguard killed during 'assassination attempt'*. Retrieved from https://www.dispatchlive.co.za/news/2023-01-07-breaking-fort-hare-vice-chancellors-bodyguard-killed-during-assassination-attempt/

   Surviving a University Department from Hell

What is happening at South African universities? The reader might ask this question. Well, the simple answer is that the criminal elements have found a soft spot in society and have literally waltzed into universities. However, criminal gangs are being aided and abetted by corrupt university officials. When closely examining some of the corrupt practices and other malfeasance I have highlighted in this book, my main conclusion is that some people want to cut corners in the academic arena and do not want to work hard to get their degrees or earn their promotions on merit. It is about jobs for pals or dishing out favours in the form of degrees, which some individuals did not earn, or awarding promotions to those who do the bidding of some senior managers and so on.

While citizens are busy pointing fingers at corrupt politicians, and rightly so, or bemoaning the rot in the country, which is perpetrated, according to them, by mostly crooked politicians, not many people are asking hard questions in relation to corruption at universities and institutions of higher learning. I hear some sections of South Africa declare unequivocally how South Africa is not a failed state. Others remind us of failed states in Africa. Well, South Africa can easily become a failed state if corruption and all forms of maleficence are not rooted out before they suffocate the entire higher education sector. Once the majority of degree holders are functional illiterates in South Africa, because of being educated and trained in institutions that are defined by corruption and criminality, then the country will surely be on its way to becoming a failed state.

Also, the country has a problem of racism which is smothering higher education and the whole of society. We should not be discussing racism almost thirty years into democracy in the manner we used to in the 1980s! We cannot allow racists to be protected and rewarded by universities. That is why I am inclined to believe that the rot at universities and institutions of higher learning is much too deep and wide for the DHEI to probe alone. I think this matter needs the urgent attention of President Matamela Cyril Ramaphosa.

In my opinion, a commission of enquiry, along the lines of the Zondo Commission,[36] which investigated state capture, corruption and all manner of wrongdoing in the public sector, should be constituted to deal with the challenges at universities and institutions of higher education. There must be a comprehensive and deep probe into all the mischief at universities, otherwise the country will surely soon be a failed state.

This book tells my personal story at a university that is supposed to be the leading university in Africa. It is not purporting to be a martyr's treatise or trying to paint the author as a saint. It stems from the premise of what South Africans refer to as *gatvol*![37]

---

36 In June 2022, Chief Justice Raymond Zondo handed the final report of the Zondo Commission to President Cyril Ramaphosa. The report was the culmination of nearly four years of investigation into state capture in South Africa by the Commission, which is officially known as the Judicial Commission of Inquiry into Allegations of State Capture. See this summary, which was produced by Devi Pillay at the Public Affairs Research Institute (PARI) in 2022: https://pari.org.za/wp-content/uploads/2022/09/PARI-Summary-The-Zondo-Commission-A-bite-sized-summary-v360.pdf
Also, see the website of the Judicial Commission of Inquiry into Allegations of State Capture, Corruption, and Fraud in the Public Sector including Organs of State. Follow this link: https://www.statecapture.org.za/

37 This is an Afrikaans word which refers to a situation when a person is simply so fed up with something or someone or extremely upset with something or someone.

     Surviving a University Department from Hell

Some people might think that I have killed my academic career by exposing the rot at UCT. Well, so be it! I was not going to be happy with myself while sitting in another little university department and knowing fully that such wrong things were being nurtured and provided oxygen at a so-called Number One University in Africa! I was not going to be true to myself.

In Africa, we need to stand up for what we believe in and especially to stand up for the right things! We cannot continue and must not celebrate wrong things in Africa. We cannot allow a situation in South Africa where whistle blowers or those who tell the truth while exposing criminal acts, are hunted down by criminals, and gunned down like animals. No! We cannot allow that. We cannot allow criminals who raped and murdered innocent souls to be turned into "pop icons" in South Africa, when the families of the deceased and survivors of heinous crimes are still reeling and coming to terms with the loss or maiming of their loved ones! No, we cannot continue to eulogise wrong things and must not condone wrong things in South Africa and Africa!